GHOST HABITS

Self-Denial of Bad Habits

Identifying Subconscious Bad Habits and Taking Baby Steps to Correct These Habits

Dr. Steve Miller

Table of Contents

Chapter 1: Understanding Ghost Habits

Introduction to Ghost Habits

Defining Ghost Habits

Ghost habits are the elusive, often unnoticed behaviors that have woven themselves into the fabric of our daily lives. These are the routines, reactions, and responses that we execute almost automatically, without conscious thought or intention. Unlike habits that we acknowledge and sometimes even celebrate—like going for a jog every morning or brushing our teeth before bed—ghost habits reside in the shadows of our awareness. They are the actions we perform on autopilot, guided by subconscious cues and unexamined beliefs.

To truly grasp the concept of ghost habits, it's essential to delve into the nature of habits themselves. A habit is a regular practice or tendency, especially one that is hard to give up. Habits form as a result of repetition and are reinforced over time until they become ingrained in our behavior. These habits are often triggered by specific cues—external or internal stimuli that prompt the habitual behavior. For instance, the ringing of an alarm clock could signal the start of your morning routine, prompting you to wake up, while simply seeing a snack might lead to eating out of habit, even if you're not actually hungry.

Ghost habits, however, are a more subtle breed of habit. They are typically born from repeated actions that initially had a purpose or were a response to a specific situation but have since lost their original context. Over time, these actions become so routine that they slip under the radar of our conscious awareness. For instance, consider someone who developed the habit of checking their phone every time they felt bored or anxious. Initially, this might have been a coping mechanism for dealing with discomfort. But over time, it turns into a ghost habit—a mindless scroll through social media whenever there's a lull, without any real intention or satisfaction.

The Unseen Forces of Ghost Habits

One of the most intriguing aspects of ghost habits is their ability to persist without us even realizing they exist. This persistence is largely due to the fact that ghost habits are deeply embedded in the subconscious mind. The subconscious is a powerful force that governs much of our behavior, often without our conscious input. It's where our beliefs, memories, and learned behaviors reside, and it's responsible for many of the automatic processes that keep us functioning day to day.

Ghost habits thrive in the subconscious because they don't require active thought to be executed. They bypass the critical thinking part of the brain, slipping through the cracks of our awareness. This is why it's common to realize only in hindsight that we've engaged in a ghost habit. You might catch yourself halfway through a bag of chips before you even realize you've started eating, or you might find yourself on a website without recalling how you got there.

The persistence of ghost habits can also be attributed to the brain's preference for efficiency. The brain is wired to conserve energy and reduce cognitive load by automating repetitive tasks. Once a behavior has been repeated enough times, the brain relegates it to the subconscious, allowing us to perform the task without expending much mental energy. While this is advantageous for many routine activities, it also means that ghost habits can continue unchecked for years, subtly shaping our behavior without our conscious consent.

The Impact of Ghost Habits on Daily Life

The effects of ghost habits on our lives can be profound, even though they often go unnoticed. Because these habits operate below the level of conscious awareness, they can steer our actions, decisions, and emotions in ways that may not align with our true goals or values. Over time, ghost habits can accumulate, creating patterns of behavior that undermine our well-being, productivity, and relationships.

Consider the example of a ghost habit related to eating. Imagine someone who has developed the habit of snacking late at night while watching TV. Initially, this behavior might have started as a way to relax after a long day. However, over time, it becomes a ghost habit—an automatic response to the end of the day, regardless of hunger or need. The person may not even realize they're eating out of habit rather than hunger. This ghost habit can lead to weight gain, disrupted sleep, and feelings of guilt or frustration, all of which can have a negative impact on overall health and well-being.

Ghost habits can also affect our mental and emotional health. For instance, a person might have a ghost habit of negative self-talk—automatically criticizing themselves whenever they make a mistake or face a challenge. This habit of self-criticism can erode self-esteem over time, leading to a pervasive sense of inadequacy and self-doubt. Because the habit operates subconsciously, the person may not even be aware of how often they engage in negative self-talk or how deeply it affects their mental state.

In the realm of relationships, ghost habits can manifest as unintentional patterns of behavior that strain connections with others. For example, someone might have the ghost habit of interrupting others during conversations, not out of rudeness but because they're accustomed to expressing their thoughts as soon as they arise. This habit, however, can be perceived as dismissive or disrespectful, leading to tension and misunderstandings in relationships.

Recognizing and Addressing Ghost Habits

The initial step in tackling ghost habits is to become aware of their presence. Because these habits operate below the surface of conscious awareness, bringing them to light requires a deliberate effort to observe our behaviors and the triggers that set them off. Mindfulness practices, such as meditation or journaling, can be powerful tools in this process. By cultivating a greater awareness of our thoughts, emotions, and actions, we can start to identify patterns that may have previously gone unnoticed.

Once a ghost habit is identified, the next step is to explore its origins and purpose. Ask yourself: When did this habit start? What need was it originally fulfilling? Does it still serve that purpose, or has it become a mindless routine? Understanding the root cause of a ghost habit can provide valuable insights into why it persists and how it might be redirected.

Changing ghost habits requires a combination of self-awareness, intention, and patience. Because these habits are deeply ingrained, they can be challenging to shift. However, by consciously interrupting the automatic behaviors and replacing them with more intentional actions, it's possible to rewire the brain and establish new, healthier habits. For instance, if you identify a ghost habit of stress eating, you might choose to replace it with a different coping mechanism, such as going for a walk or take a moment to engage in deep breathing exercises.

Conclusion

Ghost habits are an invisible yet powerful force in our lives, influencing our behavior and decisions without our conscious awareness. By bringing these habits into the light and examining their origins and impact, we can begin to take control of our actions and align them more closely with our true goals and values. The journey of understanding and transforming ghost habits is a deeply personal one, but it's also a journey toward greater self-awareness, intentionality, and fulfillment.

Origins of Ghost Habits

The Formation of Ghost Habits

Ghost habits, those subconscious behaviors that subtly influence our daily lives, do not form overnight. Their origins are often deeply rooted in our early experiences, repeated behaviors, and the psychological mechanisms that guide our actions. Understanding how these habits form is crucial for recognizing their presence and eventually altering or eliminating them. Ghost habits are typically born from a combination of environmental influences, emotional responses, and the brain's natural inclination towards efficiency.

Early Experiences: The Seedbed of Ghost Habits

Our earliest experiences play a pivotal role in the formation of ghost habits. During childhood, our brains are highly plastic, meaning they are more adaptable and capable of forming new connections rapidly. This period is critical for learning, as we absorb information from our environment and begin to develop patterns of behavior that will follow us into adulthood. Many of these patterns become ghost habits—automatic responses that are triggered by specific stimuli.

For example, a child who grows up in a household where conflict is resolved by avoidance might develop the habit of avoiding confrontation in their own life. This behavior, initially a learned response to a particular environment, becomes ingrained over time. As the child grows into adulthood, they may continue to avoid conflict, not because they consciously choose to, but because it has become a ghost habit—an automatic behavior rooted in their early experiences.

Another common source of ghost habits in early experiences is the way we learn to cope with stress and discomfort. A child who learns to soothe themselves with food, for example, may develop a ghost habit of stress eating. This habit starts as a conscious effort to comfort oneself but gradually becomes a subconscious behavior. As an adult, the individual may find themselves reaching for snacks during stressful situations without even realizing it, perpetuating the ghost habit established in childhood.

Repetition: The Reinforcement of Ghost Habits

While early experiences lay the groundwork for ghost habits, repetition is the mechanism that reinforces them. The more frequently a behavior is repeated, the more likely it is to become automatic, slipping into the subconscious and becoming a ghost habit. Repetition strengthens the neural pathways associated with the behavior, making it easier and faster for the brain to execute the action without conscious thought.

Consider the example of a person who develops the habit of checking their phone every time they feel bored. Initially, this might be a conscious decision—a way to pass the time or distract themselves from discomfort. However, with each repetition, the behavior becomes more automatic. Over time, the person may find themselves reaching for their phone without even realizing they are doing it. This repeated action has now become a ghost habit, triggered by the feeling of boredom and executed without conscious awareness.

Repetition is particularly powerful in the formation of ghost habits because it allows behaviors to become deeply ingrained in our neural circuitry. The brain is wired to seek out patterns and automate them to conserve energy. This is why habits, once formed, can be so difficult to break. The more we repeat a behavior, the more deeply it is embedded in the brain's habitual system, making it harder to change or even recognize.

Emotional Responses: The Emotional Roots of Ghost Habits

Emotions are a significant driving force behind the formation of ghost habits. Our brains are highly attuned to emotional experiences, and we often develop habits as a way of managing or responding to our emotions. When a behavior provides emotional relief or satisfaction, it is more likely to be repeated and eventually become a ghost habit.

For instance, someone who experiences anxiety might develop the habit of biting their nails as a way to soothe themselves. Initially, this behavior is a conscious response to anxiety, providing a temporary sense of relief. However, as the behavior is repeated, it becomes automatic, with the individual biting their nails whenever they feel anxious without even realizing they are doing it. The ghost habit is now firmly established, rooted in the emotional response of anxiety.

Similarly, ghost habits can form as a way to avoid negative emotions. A person who feels overwhelmed by stress might develop the habit of procrastination as a way to avoid facing their tasks. This behavior, while initially a conscious choice, becomes automatic over time. The individual may not even realize they are procrastinating; they simply find themselves engaging in distracting activities whenever they are faced with a challenging task. This ghost habit of procrastination is driven by the desire to avoid the discomfort of stress.

Environmental Influences: The External Triggers of Ghost Habits

The environment in which we live and work can also play a significant role in the formation of ghost habits. Our surroundings often provide the cues that trigger habitual behaviors, and over time, these cues can become so ingrained that they automatically elicit the corresponding behavior without conscious thought.

For example, consider someone who works in an office where colleagues frequently take coffee breaks together. Initially, joining these breaks might be a conscious choice—an opportunity to socialize and take a break from work. However, as the behavior is repeated, it becomes automatic, with the individual finding themselves getting up for a coffee break at the same time each day without even thinking about it. The environment has provided the cue (the time of day and the social norm of taking breaks), and the behavior has become a ghost habit.

Environmental cues are particularly powerful because they are often consistent and predictable. The more often we encounter the same cue, the more likely it is to trigger the corresponding behavior. This is why ghost habits can be so difficult to break; they are reinforced by the environment in which we live, work, and interact.

The Brain's Efficiency: Automating Behavior for Survival

At the core of the formation of ghost habits is the brain's natural inclination towards efficiency. The brain is constantly seeking ways to conserve energy and reduce cognitive load, and one of the ways it does this is by automating repetitive behaviors. When a behavior is repeated often enough, the brain creates neural pathways that allow the behavior to be executed with minimal conscious effort.

This efficiency is a survival mechanism. In a world where we are constantly bombarded with information and stimuli, the brain's ability to automate routine tasks allows us to focus our mental energy on more complex and demanding activities. However, this same efficiency can also lead to the formation of ghost habits— behaviors that were once intentional but have become automatic and subconscious.

The brain's preference for efficiency is why ghost habits can persist for so long, even when they no longer serve a useful purpose. Once a behavior has been automated, it requires minimal cognitive effort to maintain, making it difficult to change. This is why many people struggle to break bad habits, even when they are aware of their existence.

Breaking the Cycle: Recognizing and Addressing Ghost Habits

Understanding the origins of ghost habits is the first step in breaking the cycle and reclaiming control over our behavior. By recognizing the early experiences, repeated behaviors, emotional responses, and environmental influences that contribute to the formation of ghost habits, we can begin to bring these automatic behaviors into conscious awareness.

Once a ghost habit is identified, it is possible to interrupt the automatic cycle and replace the habit with a more intentional behavior. This process requires mindfulness, self-reflection, and a commitment to change. By consciously observing our actions and the triggers that set them off, we can begin to rewire our brains and create new, healthier habits that align with our goals and values.

Conclusion

Ghost habits are deeply ingrained behaviors that form through a combination of early experiences, repetition, emotional responses, and environmental influences. While these habits often operate below the level of conscious awareness, their impact on our lives can be profound. By understanding the origins of ghost habits and bringing them into the light of awareness, we can begin to take control of our behavior and create positive change in our lives.

Embarking on the path to identify and overcome ghost habits can be difficult, but it ultimately fosters deeper self-awareness and significant personal development.

Identifying Your Ghost Habits

The Challenge of Recognizing Ghost Habits

Ghost habits, by their very nature, are difficult to recognize because they operate below the surface of conscious awareness. These habits are so deeply ingrained in our daily routines that we often perform them without thinking. They are the automatic responses, the behaviors that feel second nature, and the routines that have become almost invisible due to their frequency and consistency.

To identify these ghost habits, it requires a shift from autopilot to conscious awareness. This shift involves becoming more mindful of our actions, thoughts, and the triggers that lead to certain behaviors. The process of identifying ghost habits is not always straightforward, but it is essential for anyone looking to gain greater control over their behavior and make positive changes in their lives.

Techniques for Identifying Ghost Habits
Mindfulness Meditation

One of the most effective techniques for identifying ghost habits is mindfulness meditation. Mindfulness involves paying close attention to the present moment, observing your thoughts, feelings, and actions without judgment. This practice can help you become more aware of your automatic behaviors, allowing you to notice when a ghost habit is in play.

To begin, set aside a few minutes each day for mindfulness meditation. Choose a peaceful spot where you can settle down comfortably and free from any interruptions. Close your eyes and focus on your breath, noticing the sensation of air entering and leaving your body. Allow your thoughts to flow freely, coming and going as they will, without any attempt to direct or control them.

During your meditation, pay attention to any recurring thoughts or urges that arise. Do you feel the need to reach for your phone? Are you tempted to grab a snack even though you're not hungry? These impulses may be linked to ghost habits. By observing them in a state of mindfulness, you can start to recognize the triggers and patterns associated with these automatic behaviors.

Journaling

Another powerful tool for identifying ghost habits is journaling. Writing about your daily experiences, thoughts, and behaviors can help you uncover patterns that you might not otherwise notice. The act of putting your thoughts on paper allows you to reflect on your actions more objectively, making it easier to spot recurring habits.

Start by keeping a daily journal where you record your activities, thoughts, and feelings. Be as detailed as possible, noting the time of day, your environment, and any emotions you experienced. After a week or so, review your journal entries and look for patterns. Are there specific times of day when you tend to engage in certain behaviors? Do certain emotions trigger automatic responses?

For example, you might notice that you always eat something sweet after lunch, even when you're not hungry. This could be a ghost habit that developed over time as a way to satisfy a craving or provide a sense of comfort. By identifying this pattern, you can start to explore why it happens and what alternative behaviors might be more beneficial.

Behavioral Tracking

Behavioral tracking is a technique that involves monitoring your actions throughout the day to identify ghost habits. This method requires you to become a detective in your own life, observing your behavior with curiosity and attention to detail.

To start, choose a specific behavior you want to track, such as how often you check your phone, snack between meals, or procrastinate on tasks. Use a notebook or a mobile app to record each time you engage in this behavior. Note the time, location, and any thoughts or emotions you experienced at that moment.

After a few days of tracking, review your notes to see if any patterns emerge. You may find that you check your phone every time you feel bored or anxious, or that you snack whenever you're working on a difficult task. These patterns can reveal ghost habits that you were previously unaware of.

Once you've identified a ghost habit, consider what triggers it and how you feel before, during, and after the behavior. Understanding these details can help you develop strategies to interrupt the habit and replace it with a more intentional action.

Ask for Feedback

Sometimes, our ghost habits are so deeply ingrained that we can't see them ourselves, but others might notice them. Asking for feedback from trusted friends, family members, or colleagues can provide valuable insights into behaviors that you may be blind to.

Choose a few people who know you well and ask them if they've noticed any habits or patterns in your behavior that you might not be aware of. Be open to their feedback and try not to be defensive. Remember, the goal is to gain a better understanding of your ghost habits so that you can address them.

For example, a colleague might point out that you have a habit of interrupting others during meetings. You might not have realized this, but it could be a ghost habit that developed over time. With this new awareness, you can start to pay more attention to your behavior in meetings and practice waiting for others to finish speaking before you respond.

Reflection and Self-Inquiry

Reflection and self-inquiry involve asking yourself probing questions to uncover the deeper reasons behind your behaviors. This technique requires honesty and a willingness to explore your thoughts and actions without judgment.

Set aside time each day or week to reflect on your behaviors and ask yourself questions like:

- Why do I engage in this behavior?

- What need or desire does this habit fulfill?

- When did I first start doing this, and why?

- How do I feel before, during, and after this behavior?

- What might happen if I didn't engage in this habit?

You can explore these questions to identify the root causes and motivations behind your ghost habits For example, you might discover that your habit of staying up late every night started as a way to carve out personal time after a busy day. Recognizing this can help you explore healthier ways to meet that need without sacrificing sleep.

Exercises for Identifying Ghost Habits

Habit Audit

A habit audit is a comprehensive exercise that involves reviewing all aspects of your daily routine to identify ghost habits. This exercise requires you to examine your day from start to finish, noting every habitual action you take.

To perform a habit audit, begin by meticulously documenting every activity you undertake throughout the day, starting from the moment you wake up until the time you go to sleep. Make sure to include every action, regardless of how minor or routine it may appear. For example, brushing your teeth, checking your phone, drinking coffee, taking a shower, and commuting to work should all be included.

Once you've listed all your activities, go through each one and ask yourself if it's a conscious choice or an automatic behavior. If it's automatic, consider whether it's serving a positive purpose or if it might be a ghost habit that's no longer beneficial.

For each ghost habit you identify, write down when and why it started, how it makes you feel, and what triggers it. This will help you build a clearer picture of your ghost habits and how they influence your daily life.

Trigger Analysis

Trigger analysis is an exercise that focuses on identifying the specific cues that activate your ghost habits. By understanding what triggers a habit, you can begin to interrupt the automatic response and replace it with a more intentional action.

To perform trigger analysis, choose a habit you want to explore and keep track of every time you engage in it over the course of a week. Each time the habit occurs, note the following:

- The time of day
- The location
- Who you were with (if anyone)
- What you were doing just before the habit occurred
- How you were feeling emotionally and physically

After a week, review your notes to identify common triggers. You might find that certain times of day, environments, or emotional states consistently lead to the habit. For example, you might discover that you always reach for a snack at 3 p.m. when you're feeling bored at work.

With this information, you can start to develop strategies to address the trigger before the habit occurs. In the case of the 3 p.m. snack, you might decide to take a quick walk or stretch break to combat boredom instead of reaching for food.

Conclusion

Identifying ghost habits is a crucial step toward greater self-awareness and personal growth. By using techniques like mindfulness meditation, journaling, behavioral tracking, asking for feedback, and reflection, you can begin to recognize the automatic behaviors that shape your daily life. Exercises such as habit audits and trigger analysis further aid in uncovering these subconscious patterns, allowing you to take control of your actions and make more intentional choices. The journey to identifying and transforming ghost habits may be challenging, but it is a powerful way to align your behavior with your goals and values, ultimately leading to a more fulfilling life.

Chapter 2: The Power of Self-Denial

What is Self-Denial?

Understanding the Concept of Self-Denial

Self-denial is a powerful and often misunderstood concept that plays a crucial role in personal development, especially when it comes to overcoming bad habits. At its core, self-denial involves the conscious decision to resist or forgo certain desires, impulses, or behaviors that may be harmful or counterproductive. It is the ability to say "no" to oneself in the pursuit of a greater goal, higher values, or long-term well-being.

In everyday life, self-denial can manifest in various forms, from simple acts of willpower, like resisting the temptation to indulge in unhealthy foods, to more profound sacrifices, such as abstaining from harmful habits or behaviors that negatively impact one's life. Self-denial is not about deprivation or punishment; rather, it is about exercising control over one's impulses and making choices that align with one's values and long-term goals.

In the context of bad habits, self-denial is an essential tool for breaking free from patterns of behavior that are detrimental to one's physical, mental, or emotional health. Bad habits are often the result of succumbing to immediate gratification or comfort, even when the long-term consequences are harmful. Self-denial empowers individuals to overcome these habits by fostering a mindset of discipline, self-control, and intentionality.

The Role of Self-Denial in Overcoming Bad Habits

Bad habits are behaviors that have become ingrained over time, often through repetition and reinforcement. These habits can range from relatively benign actions, such as procrastination, to more destructive behaviors, like smoking, excessive drinking, or overeating. What makes bad habits particularly challenging to overcome is their ability to provide immediate satisfaction or relief, even when the long-term consequences are negative.

This is where self-denial comes into play. By practicing self-denial, individuals can interrupt the cycle of immediate gratification that fuels bad habits. Instead of giving in to the impulse to engage in a harmful behavior, self-denial encourages a pause—a moment of reflection where one can consider the consequences of their actions and make a conscious decision to act in a way that supports their long-term goals.

For example, consider someone who is trying to quit smoking. The urge to smoke might be strong, especially in situations that trigger stress or anxiety. However, by practicing self-denial, the individual can resist the immediate temptation to light a cigarette, recognizing that the short-term relief is outweighed by the long-term harm to their health. In this way, self-denial becomes a powerful tool for breaking the habit and moving towards a healthier lifestyle.

Self-denial is not about suppressing desires or emotions; rather, it is about redirecting them in a way that aligns with one's values and aspirations. It involves acknowledging the presence of a desire or impulse but choosing not to act on it in the moment. Over time, this practice can help to weaken the grip of bad habits, making it easier to adopt new, more positive behaviors.

The Psychological Basis of Self-Denial

The concept of self-denial is deeply rooted in psychology, particularly in the study of self-control and willpower. Research has shown that self-control is like a muscle—it can be strengthened with practice but also fatigued by overuse. This means that self-denial, when practiced regularly, can become a more natural and automatic response, making it easier to resist temptations and break bad habits.

One of the key psychological principles behind self-denial is delayed gratification—the ability to resist an immediate reward in favor of a greater reward in the future. In the 1960s, psychologist Walter Mischel conducted what has become known as the renowned "marshmallow experiment," a pivotal study that exemplifies this concept.. In the experiment, children were given the choice to eat one marshmallow immediately or wait for a period of time and receive two marshmallows. The study found that children who were able to delay gratification tended to have better life outcomes, including higher academic achievement and better health.

Self-denial is essentially the practice of delaying gratification in everyday life. It requires individuals to think beyond the present moment and consider the long-term consequences of their actions. This shift in focus from immediate pleasure to long-term well-being is at the heart of self-denial and is a critical component in overcoming bad habits.

Another important psychological aspect of self-denial is the concept of cognitive reframing. This involves changing the way one thinks about a particular behavior or situation in order to alter its perceived value. For example, instead of viewing self-denial as a form of deprivation, individuals can reframe it as an act of self-care and empowerment. By shifting the focus from what is being denied to what is being gained (e.g., better health, greater self-esteem, improved relationships), self-denial becomes a positive and motivating force.

Practical Strategies for Practicing Self-Denial

While the concept of self-denial is simple, putting it into practice can be challenging, especially when dealing with deeply ingrained bad habits. However, there are several strategies that can help individuals develop the habit of self-denial and make it a more integral part of their daily lives.

- *Set Clear Goals and Priorities*

One of the most effective ways to practice self-denial is to have a clear understanding of your goals and priorities. When you know what you are working towards, it becomes easier to resist behaviors that are counterproductive to those goals. Take the time to identify what is most important to you—whether it's improving your health, strengthening relationships, advancing your career, or achieving personal growth. Keep these priorities in mind when faced with temptations, and remind yourself that self-denial is a step towards achieving your goals.

- *Create a Plan for Managing Temptations*

Temptations are inevitable, especially when trying to break a bad habit. Having a plan in place for how to handle these temptations can make it easier to practice self-denial in the moment. This plan might include strategies like removing triggers from your environment, finding alternative activities to distract yourself, or practicing mindfulness to stay present and focused on your goals. The key is to be proactive and have a strategy ready for when temptation strikes.

- *Practice Self-Denial in Small Steps*

Building the habit of self-denial doesn't happen overnight. It requires consistent practice, starting with small, manageable steps. Begin by identifying one or two areas in your life where you can practice self-denial. For example, you might start by resisting the urge to check your phone during meals or by cutting back on sugary snacks. As you build confidence and strength in these areas, gradually expand your practice of self-denial to other aspects of your life.

- *Use Positive Reinforcement*

Self-denial can be challenging, but it doesn't have to be unpleasant. One way to make the process more enjoyable is to use positive reinforcement. Reward yourself for successfully practicing self-denial, whether it's by treating yourself to something you enjoy or simply acknowledging your progress. Positive reinforcement can help to build a positive association with self-denial, making it easier to continue practicing it over time.

- *Reflect on Your Progress*

Regular reflection is an important part of practicing self-denial. Take the time to assess your progress, noting any successes as well as areas where you struggled. Use this reflection to learn from your experiences and make adjustments to your strategies as needed. Over time, this process of reflection and adjustment will help you to strengthen your ability to practice self-denial and achieve your goals.

Conclusion

Self-denial is a powerful tool for overcoming bad habits and achieving personal growth. By understanding the concept of self-denial and its role in breaking the cycle of immediate gratification, individuals can develop greater self-control and intentionality in their actions. Through the practice of self-denial, it is possible to align one's behavior with long-term goals and values, leading to a more fulfilling and purposeful life. While the journey of self-denial may be challenging, it is ultimately a journey of empowerment and transformation, offering the opportunity to take control of one's habits and shape a better future.

Why We Deny Our Habits

The Complexity of Habit Denial

Denying our habits, especially those that are harmful, is a complex psychological phenomenon. It's not just about ignoring or refusing to acknowledge certain behaviors; it's a deeper, often subconscious process where we protect ourselves from the discomfort of facing truths that may be difficult to accept. The denial of habits, particularly bad ones, can stem from a variety of psychological and emotional reasons, each deeply intertwined with our self-perception, emotional coping mechanisms, and the inherent difficulty of change.

The Role of Cognitive Dissonance

One of the primary psychological reasons behind habit denial is cognitive dissonance, a term coined by psychologist Leon Festinger. Cognitive dissonance occurs when there is a conflict between our beliefs, values, and actions. When we engage in behaviors that contradict our self-image or beliefs, it creates a sense of discomfort. To alleviate this discomfort, the mind often resorts to denial as a defense mechanism.

For example, someone who considers themselves health-conscious might struggle to acknowledge their habit of smoking. The act of smoking directly contradicts their self-image as a person who cares about their health. Rather than facing this inconsistency, which would require them to either quit smoking or adjust their self-perception, the individual may deny the significance of their smoking habit. They might downplay the risks, justify the behavior as a temporary indulgence, or even convince themselves that they are in control and can quit anytime. This denial serves to protect their self-image and reduce the psychological discomfort caused by the dissonance.

Emotional Avoidance and Comfort

Emotional avoidance is another significant factor in the denial of habits. Many bad habits are rooted in emotional states—such as stress, anxiety, sadness, or boredom—that we seek to alleviate. These habits often provide temporary comfort or distraction from unpleasant emotions. Acknowledging these habits would force us to confront the underlying emotional issues, which can be daunting or overwhelming.

For instance, a person who overeats when they are stressed may deny that their eating habits are problematic. Admitting to overeating would require them to confront their stress and find healthier ways to cope, which might feel more challenging than simply continuing the behavior. The habit, in this case, serves as a form of emotional self-medication, and denial becomes a way to avoid the pain of dealing with the underlying stress.

Moreover, the immediate gratification provided by bad habits reinforces their continued existence. The pleasure or relief we get from these habits, even if fleeting, can create a cycle where the habit is repeated to avoid negative emotions. Over time, this can lead to a deep-seated denial, as admitting the habit would mean losing a familiar and reliable (though ultimately harmful) coping mechanism.

Fear of Change and the Unknown

Change, even when necessary, is inherently difficult. It requires us to step out of our comfort zones and face uncertainty. This fear of change is a powerful motivator for denying our bad habits. Acknowledging a bad habit often implies that we need to take steps to change it, which can feel overwhelming or frightening. The unknown outcomes of change—whether we will succeed, how our lives will be different, and how others might react—can create significant anxiety.

This fear is particularly strong when the habit has been part of our lives for a long time. The habit, no matter how detrimental, has become a known quantity, something predictable in an unpredictable world. Admitting the need to change it means stepping into a space of vulnerability and uncertainty, where there are no guarantees. To avoid this discomfort, people may deny the existence or seriousness of their bad habits, convincing themselves that change is unnecessary or that the habit is not as harmful as it seems.

Social and Cultural Influences

Our social environment and cultural background also play a significant role in the denial of habits. We are influenced by the norms and expectations of the society we live in, and these can shape our perceptions of what is acceptable or unacceptable behavior. If a particular habit is socially accepted or even encouraged, it can be easier to deny its negative impact on our lives.

For example, in a culture where heavy drinking is normalized as part of social interaction, an individual might deny that their drinking habits are problematic. They may justify their behavior by pointing to others who drink just as much, or they might convince themselves that their drinking is a necessary part of fitting in socially. The broader cultural acceptance of the habit makes it easier to deny its potential harm.

Similarly, the pressure to conform to social norms can lead to the denial of habits that might be perceived as socially unacceptable. For instance, someone who struggles with compulsive shopping may deny their habit because it conflicts with the societal expectation of financial responsibility. The fear of judgment or stigma can drive the person to downplay or rationalize their behavior, rather than confront it openly.

The Illusion of Control

One frequent cause of habit denial is the mistaken belief that we have complete control over our actions. People often convince themselves that they have control over their bad habits, even when the evidence suggests otherwise. This belief allows them to minimize the significance of the habit, reassuring themselves that they can stop at any time.

For example, a person with a gambling habit might deny that it's a problem by telling themselves that they can quit whenever they want, or that they are simply enjoying a harmless pastime. This illusion of control provides a comforting narrative that allows them to continue the behavior without acknowledging the potential risks.

The illusion of control is particularly dangerous because it can lead to the escalation of bad habits. As the habit becomes more ingrained, the individual may continue to deny its impact, believing they are still in control even as the consequences become more severe. This denial can prevent them from seeking help or taking action until the habit has caused significant damage to their life.

The Comfort of Familiarity

Familiarity is another powerful reason why people deny their bad habits. Human beings are creatures of habit, and we find comfort in routines and behaviors that are predictable and consistent. Even when a habit is harmful, its familiarity can make it difficult to let go. The thought of changing a well-established routine can create anxiety, leading to denial as a way to avoid the discomfort of change.

This is particularly true for habits that have been part of a person's life for many years. The longer a habit has been in place, the more integrated it becomes into the individual's identity and daily life. Denying the need to change the habit can be a way to preserve the sense of stability and predictability that the habit provides, even if it is ultimately detrimental.

Defense Mechanisms and Self-Protection

Denial is one of the most common defense mechanisms that the mind employs to protect itself from psychological distress. Sigmund Freud, the father of psychoanalysis, identified denial as a way for the ego to defend itself against anxiety and maintain psychological equilibrium. When faced with a reality that is too painful or threatening to accept, the mind may choose to deny or distort that reality.

In the context of bad habits, denial serves as a way to protect oneself from the guilt, shame, or fear that might come with acknowledging the habit. For example, someone who has developed a habit of lying may deny that they have a problem because admitting it would mean confronting the ethical and relational implications of their behavior. The denial allows them to avoid these uncomfortable emotions and maintain their self-image.

The Role of Self-Compassion in Overcoming Denial

While denial can be a significant barrier to overcoming bad habits, it is not insurmountable. One of the most effective ways to move beyond denial is through self-compassion. Self-compassion involves treating oneself with kindness, understanding, and acceptance, particularly in moments of failure or difficulty.

When we approach our habits with self-compassion, we create a safe space to explore our behaviors without judgment or shame. This openness allows us to acknowledge our habits honestly and consider the underlying reasons for them. Instead of denying our habits, we can begin to understand them and take steps toward positive change.

Self-compassion also helps to reduce the fear of change and the associated anxiety. By recognizing that change is a process and that it's okay to struggle along the way, we can reduce the need for denial and take more proactive steps toward transforming our habits.

Conclusion

The denial of bad habits is a complex and multifaceted phenomenon driven by psychological and emotional factors such as cognitive dissonance, emotional avoidance, fear of change, social influences, the illusion of control, and the comfort of familiarity. Recognizing the deeper causes behind our actions allows us to identify moments when denial might be influencing our decisions and behaviors.. By cultivating self-awareness and self-compassion, we can break through the barriers of denial, confront our habits honestly, and take meaningful steps toward personal growth and positive change.

The Consequences of Ignoring Ghost Habits

The Invisible Influence of Ghost Habits

Ghost habits, those deeply ingrained and often subconscious behaviors that guide much of our daily lives, can have a profound impact when left unexamined and unchecked. While they may seem harmless or even go unnoticed, the consequences of ignoring ghost habits can be far-reaching, affecting various aspects of our lives. Denial of these habits not only reinforces negative patterns but also significantly hinders personal growth, keeping us trapped in cycles that limit our potential and well-being.

The Reinforcement of Negative Patterns

At the heart of ghost habits is their ability to operate below the level of conscious awareness. These habits often develop over time, becoming automatic responses to certain triggers or situations. Because they are so deeply embedded, we may not recognize them as problematic, even when they are causing harm. This is where denial comes into play. By refusing to acknowledge the existence or impact of these habits, we allow them to persist, reinforcing the very patterns that keep us stuck.

Consider the example of someone who has developed a ghost habit of procrastination. This person may repeatedly delay important tasks, telling themselves they work better under pressure or that they'll get to it later. Over time, this habit becomes ingrained, leading to a cycle of last-minute rushes, missed opportunities, and increased stress. By denying that procrastination is a problem, the individual continues to reinforce this negative pattern, making it harder to break free.

Denial serves as a protective mechanism, allowing us to avoid the discomfort of confronting our habits. However, this avoidance only strengthens the habits' hold on us. The more we deny the existence or severity of a ghost habit, the more entrenched it becomes, creating a self-perpetuating cycle that is difficult to escape. As a result, negative patterns become deeply rooted in our behavior, shaping our decisions, actions, and outcomes.

The Erosion of Self-Awareness

One of the most significant consequences of ignoring ghost habits is the erosion of self-awareness. Self-awareness is the foundation of personal growth; it involves understanding our thoughts, emotions, and behaviors, and how they influence our lives. When we ignore ghost habits, we lose touch with this crucial aspect of ourselves.

Ghost habits, by their very nature, operate without our conscious input. When we fail to recognize and address them, we allow these habits to guide our actions without questioning their validity or impact. Over time, this lack of awareness can lead to a disconnect between our actions and our true intentions or values. We may find ourselves engaging in behaviors that don't align with who we want to be, yet remain unaware of why we're doing so.

For example, someone who has a ghost habit of negative self-talk may consistently criticize themselves without realizing the toll it takes on their self-esteem and mental health. Because this habit operates subconsciously, the individual may not be fully aware of the extent to which their inner dialogue is affecting their well-being. By ignoring this habit, they miss the opportunity to develop greater self-compassion and to challenge the negative beliefs that fuel their self-criticism.

The erosion of self-awareness not only hampers personal growth but also makes it more difficult to make intentional, positive changes in our lives. Without awareness, we are more likely to remain on autopilot, repeating the same behaviors and making the same choices without understanding why. This lack of insight prevents us from taking control of our lives and making decisions that truly reflect our values and goals.

The Impact on Personal Relationships

Ignoring ghost habits doesn't just affect our personal development; it can also have a significant impact on our relationships with others. Many ghost habits involve behaviors that, while seemingly insignificant, can create tension, misunderstandings, or conflict in our interactions with others.

For instance, someone with a ghost habit of interrupting others in conversation may not realize how this behavior affects their relationships. They may see it as a harmless quirk or a sign of enthusiasm, but to others, it may come across as disrespectful or dismissive. By denying that this habit is problematic, the individual fails to address the impact it has on their relationships, potentially leading to resentment or a breakdown in communication.

Similarly, ghost habits related to emotional expression can strain relationships. A person who habitually suppresses their emotions may struggle to connect with others on a deeper level. They may avoid discussing their feelings or dismiss the emotions of others, creating a barrier to intimacy and understanding. By ignoring this ghost habit, they miss the opportunity to develop more meaningful and supportive relationships.

The denial of ghost habits in relationships can lead to a cycle of negative interactions, where the same issues continue to arise without resolution. Over time, this can gradually undermine trust, hinder effective communication, and diminish mutual respect, creating significant obstacles in developing and sustaining healthy, satisfying relationships..

The Stagnation of Personal Growth

Personal growth is a continuous process that involves learning, evolving, and becoming the best version of ourselves. However, when we ignore ghost habits, we hinder this process, leading to stagnation and a lack of progress in our personal development.

Ghost habits often act as barriers to growth by keeping us within our comfort zones. These habits are familiar and predictable, providing a sense of security even when they are harmful. By denying their existence, we avoid the discomfort of change, choosing instead to remain in a state of inertia. This stagnation prevents us from taking the risks necessary for growth, such as trying new things, challenging our beliefs, or stepping outside our usual patterns of behavior.

For example, someone with a ghost habit of avoiding new experiences may miss out on opportunities for personal growth. They may tell themselves that they are content with their current routine or that they don't need to step outside their comfort zone. However, this denial keeps them from exploring new possibilities, learning new skills, or gaining new perspectives that could enrich their lives.

The stagnation caused by ignoring ghost habits can also manifest in a lack of fulfillment or purpose. When we fail to address the habits that hold us back, we may find ourselves stuck in unfulfilling jobs, relationships, or lifestyles, unable to make the changes needed to achieve greater satisfaction and meaning. This sense of being stuck can lead to frustration, dissatisfaction, and a feeling of being trapped in a life that doesn't reflect our true potential.

The Long-Term Consequences on Mental and Physical Health

The denial of ghost habits can have serious long-term consequences for both mental and physical health. Many ghost habits involve behaviors that, while seemingly harmless in the short term, can lead to significant health issues if left unaddressed.

For instance, someone with a ghost habit of stress eating may not realize the impact it has on their physical health over time. By denying that this habit is a problem, they may continue to consume unhealthy foods in response to stress, leading to weight gain, digestive issues, and an increased risk of chronic diseases like diabetes or heart disease. The long-term consequences of ignoring this habit can be severe, yet the individual may not recognize the need for change until it's too late.

Similarly, ghost habits related to mental health, such as avoiding stress or anxiety, can have detrimental effects. A person who consistently avoids confronting stress might resort to unhealthy coping strategies such as indulging in alcohol, substance use, or spending excessive time on digital devices. Over time, these habits can lead to mental health issues such as depression, anxiety disorders, or addiction. The denial of these habits prevents the individual from seeking help or developing healthier coping strategies, leading to a decline in overall well-being.

Ignoring ghost habits can also exacerbate existing mental health conditions. For example, someone with a ghost habit of perfectionism may constantly set unrealistic standards for themselves, leading to chronic stress, burnout, and feelings of inadequacy. By denying the impact of this habit, they may continue to push themselves to the brink, unaware of the toll it's taking on their mental health.

Breaking the Cycle: The Importance of Awareness and Action

The consequences of ignoring ghost habits are clear: they reinforce negative patterns, erode self-awareness, strain relationships, stagnate personal growth, and harm mental and physical health. However, these consequences are not inevitable. By bringing ghost habits into the light of awareness and taking action to address them, we can break the cycle and create positive change in our lives.

The first step in breaking the cycle is to cultivate self-awareness. This involves paying attention to our thoughts, feelings, and behaviors, and being honest with ourselves about the habits that may be holding us back. Mindfulness practices, journaling, and seeking feedback from others can all help to increase awareness of ghost habits.

Once we've identified our ghost habits, the next step is to take action. This might involve setting specific goals for change, seeking support from friends, family, or professionals, and developing new, healthier habits to replace the old ones. The process of change can be challenging, but it is essential for personal growth and well-being.

Conclusion

Ignoring ghost habits can have significant consequences, reinforcing negative patterns and hindering personal growth. By denying these habits, we allow them to shape our lives in ways that limit our potential and harm our well-being. However, by cultivating self-awareness and taking proactive steps to address our ghost habits, we can break free from these negative patterns and create a life that is more aligned with our true values, goals, and aspirations. The journey of confronting and transforming ghost habits is a powerful step towards greater self-awareness, fulfillment, and personal growth.

Chapter 3: Identifying Subconscious Triggers

Understanding Subconscious Triggers

Defining Subconscious Triggers

Subconscious triggers are the underlying cues that prompt our behaviors, thoughts, and emotions without our conscious awareness. These triggers operate below the surface of our conscious mind, influencing our actions in ways we may not fully realize. Unlike conscious triggers, which are readily identifiable and deliberate, subconscious triggers are subtle and often stem from deeply ingrained experiences, beliefs, or emotions. They can be powerful forces that drive our habits, shape our responses, and even dictate how we interact with the world around us.

Subconscious triggers are rooted in the complex workings of the brain, particularly in areas responsible for automatic processing and emotional regulation. These triggers can be anything from sensory stimuli, like a particular smell or sound, to internal states, such as stress or fatigue. Because they bypass our conscious thought processes, we may find ourselves reacting in certain ways without understanding why. Recognizing and understanding these triggers is a crucial step in gaining control over our behaviors and making more intentional choices in our lives.

How Subconscious Triggers Influence Behavior

The influence of subconscious triggers on behavior is profound. These triggers act as invisible forces that shape our actions, often leading us to repeat certain behaviors without conscious deliberation. The process by which subconscious triggers influence behavior can be understood through the framework of classical conditioning, a concept in psychology that explains how certain stimuli become associated with specific responses.

In classical conditioning, an initially neutral stimulus becomes associated with a particular response through repeated pairing with a stimulus that naturally elicits that response. Over time, the neutral stimulus by itself can begin to evoke the same response, even without the presence of the original stimulus. This learned association becomes a subconscious trigger, automatically prompting the behavior whenever the trigger is encountered.

For example, imagine someone who always eats popcorn while watching movies. Initially, the act of watching a movie may have had no direct connection to eating popcorn. However, after repeated experiences where popcorn was consumed during movies, the sight of a movie screen may become a subconscious trigger for the craving to eat popcorn. The individual might find themselves reaching for popcorn whenever they start a movie, even if they're not particularly hungry. The movie has become a subconscious trigger, influencing behavior without the need for conscious thought.

Subconscious triggers can also be linked to emotional states. For instance, someone who turns to food for comfort during times of stress may develop a subconscious trigger where the feeling of stress automatically leads to the desire to eat. The stress acts as a trigger, and the behavior—eating—becomes an automatic response. Over time, this pattern can become so ingrained that the individual is not even aware of the connection between their emotional state and their eating habits.

The Role of the Brain in Subconscious Triggering

The brain plays a central role in the formation and activation of subconscious triggers. Several key brain structures are involved in processing and responding to these triggers, including the amygdala, hippocampus, and prefrontal cortex. These areas work together to encode, store, and retrieve the associations that form the basis of subconscious triggers.

The amygdala, a small almond-shaped structure located deep within the brain, is primarily responsible for processing emotions, particularly those related to fear and pleasure. The amygdala is highly sensitive to emotional stimuli and plays a key role in the formation of emotional memories. When a behavior or response is consistently paired with a strong emotional experience, the amygdala helps to encode this association, making it more likely that the behavior will be triggered subconsciously in the future.

The hippocampus, another important brain structure, is involved in memory formation and retrieval. It works closely with the amygdala to store and recall the associations between stimuli and responses. The hippocampus helps to create a mental map of our experiences, linking specific triggers to particular behaviors or emotions. When a familiar trigger is encountered, the hippocampus retrieves the associated memory, prompting the corresponding behavior or response.

The prefrontal cortex, located at the front of the brain, is responsible for higher-level cognitive functions, such as decision-making, planning, and self-regulation. While the prefrontal cortex is involved in conscious thought processes, it also interacts with the amygdala and hippocampus to influence our responses to subconscious triggers. In some cases, the prefrontal cortex may help to override automatic responses, allowing us to make more deliberate choices. However, when subconscious triggers are strong and deeply ingrained, they can bypass the prefrontal cortex, leading to automatic behaviors that occur without conscious control.

Examples of Subconscious Triggers in Everyday Life

Subconscious triggers are pervasive in everyday life, influencing a wide range of behaviors, from the mundane to the significant. Recognizing these triggers can help us better understand why we act the way we do and how we can make changes to improve our behavior and well-being.

One common example of a subconscious trigger is the association between time and certain activities. Many people have specific routines or habits that are triggered by the time of day. For instance, someone might have a habit of drinking coffee every morning at 8:00 a.m. Over time, the mere sight of the clock at 8:00 a.m. may trigger a craving for coffee, even if they are not particularly tired or in need of caffeine. The time of day has become a subconscious trigger for the behavior of drinking coffee.

Another example is the way certain environments can act as subconscious triggers. For instance, someone who frequently snacks while watching TV may find that sitting on the couch in front of the television automatically triggers the desire to eat, even if they are not hungry. The environment—the couch and the TV— has become associated with the behavior of snacking, leading to an automatic response whenever the person is in that setting.

Subconscious triggers can also be linked to social interactions. For example, someone who feels anxious in social situations may develop a habit of avoiding eye contact or fidgeting when they are around others. These behaviors may be triggered automatically whenever they are in a social setting, without the person consciously deciding to act that way. The presence of other people becomes a subconscious trigger for the behavior of avoiding eye contact or fidgeting.

The Impact of Subconscious Triggers on Habits

Subconscious triggers are a key factor in the development and maintenance of habits, both positive and negative. Because these triggers operate automatically, they can make it difficult to change behaviors, even when we are aware that the behavior is harmful or undesirable.

For instance, someone who has developed a habit of smoking in response to stress may find it challenging to quit, even if they consciously want to stop. The stress acts as a powerful subconscious trigger, automatically prompting the desire to smoke. Each time the individual experiences stress, the trigger is activated, making it difficult to resist the urge to smoke. The automatic nature of the trigger-response cycle reinforces the habit, making it more entrenched over time.

The influence of subconscious triggers on habits is also evident in the way certain cues can lead to cravings or urges. For example, someone who is trying to cut back on sugary foods may find that walking past a bakery triggers a strong desire for sweets. The sight and smell of the baked goods act as subconscious triggers, automatically prompting the craving for sugar. Even if the person is not hungry or consciously thinking about sweets, the trigger is powerful enough to influence their behavior, potentially leading them to give in to the craving.

Strategies for Identifying and Managing Subconscious Triggers

Understanding the role of subconscious triggers in behavior is an important step in gaining control over our habits and making positive changes. However, because these triggers operate below the level of conscious awareness, identifying and managing them can be challenging. Fortunately, there are several strategies that can help bring subconscious triggers to light and reduce their influence on behavior.

- *Mindfulness and Self-Reflection*

Practicing mindfulness and self-reflection can help increase awareness of subconscious triggers. By paying close attention to your thoughts, emotions, and behaviors, you can begin to notice patterns and identify the triggers that prompt certain actions. Mindfulness involves staying present in the moment and observing your experiences without judgment. Over time, this practice can help you become more attuned to the subtle cues that influence your behavior.

Self-reflection, such as journaling or talking through your experiences with a trusted friend or therapist, can also help you explore the underlying triggers for your behavior. By reflecting on your actions and the circumstances that led up to them, you can start to identify the subconscious triggers that may be at play.

- *Behavioral Tracking*

Another effective strategy for identifying subconscious triggers is behavioral tracking. This involves keeping a detailed record of your behaviors, along with any associated thoughts, emotions, and environmental cues. By tracking your behavior over time, you can start to identify patterns and uncover the triggers that may be influencing your actions.

For example, if you are trying to identify the triggers for stress eating, you might keep a journal where you record each instance of eating in response to stress. Note the time, place, emotions, and any specific events or thoughts that occurred before you ate. Over time, you may notice that certain situations, such as work deadlines or interpersonal conflicts, consistently trigger the behavior.

- *Cognitive Restructuring*

Cognitive restructuring involves challenging and changing the thoughts and beliefs that contribute to automatic behaviors. This technique can be particularly effective for managing subconscious triggers by altering the way you respond to them.

For instance, if you identify that stress is a trigger for smoking, cognitive restructuring might involve challenging the belief that smoking is the only way to cope with stress. You could work on developing alternative coping strategies, such as deep breathing, exercise, or talking to a friend, and practice these new responses when the trigger occurs. Over time, this can weaken the association between the trigger and the behavior, making it easier to resist the urge to smoke.

- *Environmental Modification*

Modifying your environment to reduce exposure to subconscious triggers can also be an effective strategy for managing behavior. If you identify certain settings or cues that consistently trigger unwanted behavior, consider making changes to your environment to minimize these triggers.

For example, if you find that you are more likely to snack mindlessly while watching TV, you might try changing your routine by watching TV in a different room, engaging in a different activity while watching, or removing unhealthy snacks from your home. By altering your environment, you can reduce the likelihood of encountering triggers and make it easier to adopt healthier behaviors.

Conclusion

Subconscious triggers are powerful forces that influence our behavior, often without our conscious awareness. These triggers can shape our habits, drive our actions, and impact our decisions in ways that are difficult to recognize or control. By understanding the nature of subconscious triggers and the role they play in our lives, we can begin to identify and manage them more effectively. Through mindfulness, self-reflection, behavioral tracking, cognitive restructuring, and environmental modification, we can bring these triggers into the light of awareness and take steps to align our behavior with our goals and values. The journey of identifying and managing subconscious triggers is a crucial step toward greater self-awareness, personal growth, and the creation of a more intentional and fulfilling life.

Common Triggers

Understanding the Power of Common Triggers

Triggers are stimuli—whether internal or external—that provoke a certain reaction or behavior, often without conscious awareness. These triggers can lead to the formation and reinforcement of ghost habits, which are subconscious routines that subtly influence our lives. Recognizing these triggers is essential for gaining insight into the reasons behind our actions and discovering effective ways to modify them.. Below are some of the most common triggers that can lead to the development of ghost habits.

- *Environmental Cues*

Our surroundings play a significant role in shaping our behaviors, often without us realizing it. Environmental cues are one of the most powerful triggers for ghost habits because they are constant and ever-present. These triggers can include specific locations, objects, or even people that are associated with certain behaviors.

For example, consider someone who has developed the habit of snacking while watching television. Over time, the act of sitting on the couch and turning on the TV becomes a subconscious trigger for eating, even when the person isn't hungry. The environment—specifically, the couch and TV—cues the behavior automatically. This trigger can become so ingrained that the person may find it difficult to watch TV without reaching for a snack, reinforcing the ghost habit.

Another example is the workplace environment. Someone who always takes a coffee break at a certain time of day may begin to associate that time and location with the need for caffeine, even if they don't feel particularly tired. The office setting and the clock become triggers that prompt the behavior of drinking coffee, turning it into a routine that happens almost without thought.

- *Emotional States*

Emotions are powerful triggers that can lead to the formation of ghost habits, especially those related to coping mechanisms. When we experience certain emotions, our brains often seek ways to manage or alleviate those feelings, leading to the development of automatic behaviors.

For instance, stress is a common emotional trigger that can lead to a variety of ghost habits. A person might reach for a cigarette, comfort food, or a drink whenever they feel stressed. Over time, the emotional state of stress becomes closely linked with these behaviors, so much so that the person may engage in them automatically whenever they feel stressed, even if they don't consciously recognize the connection.

Similarly, feelings of boredom or loneliness can trigger ghost habits like mindless scrolling through social media, binge-watching TV shows, or online shopping. These activities may initially provide a distraction or a sense of relief, but they can quickly become automatic responses to these emotions. The more these behaviors are repeated, the more they become ingrained as ghost habits triggered by these emotional states.

Social and Cultural Norms

Social and cultural influences are another set of powerful triggers that can lead to the formation of ghost habits. The expectations, behaviors, and norms of the people around us, as well as the broader culture in which we live, can shape our actions in ways we might not consciously recognize.

For example, someone who regularly goes out for drinks with colleagues after work may develop a ghost habit of drinking alcohol in social settings, even when they don't particularly want to. The social environment and cultural norm of drinking after work become triggers that prompt the behavior. This can happen without the person consciously deciding to drink; instead, they find themselves following the social script that has been laid out by their environment.

Cultural norms around food can also act as triggers. In many cultures, certain foods are associated with specific times of day or social events. Someone who grew up in a culture where dessert is always served after dinner might develop a ghost habit of craving something sweet every evening, even if they aren't hungry. The cultural norm of ending a meal with dessert often acts as an unconscious prompt, leading to the habitual consumption of sugary treats.

- *Routine and Repetition*

Routine and repetition are key factors in the formation of ghost habits. When a behavior is repeated frequently enough, it becomes automatic, and the triggers associated with that behavior become ingrained in the subconscious mind. Over time, these triggers can prompt the behavior with little or no conscious thought.

For example, someone who has developed the habit of checking their phone first thing in the morning may do so automatically every day. The routine of waking up becomes a trigger for the behavior of checking the phone, even before the person is fully awake. This ghost habit can become so ingrained that the person might find it difficult to resist the urge to check their phone, even when they know it's not necessary.

Another common example is the routine of eating at specific times of the day. Many people have established meal times—breakfast, lunch, and dinner—that they follow out of habit. The time of day becomes a trigger for eating, regardless of whether the person is actually hungry. This routine-based trigger can lead to ghost habits around food consumption, where the act of eating is more about adhering to a schedule than responding to actual hunger cues.

- *Sensory Triggers*

Sensory experiences—such as sights, sounds, smells, tastes, and textures—can also act as powerful triggers for ghost habits. These sensory triggers are closely linked to memory and emotion, making them particularly effective at prompting automatic behaviors.

For instance, the smell of freshly baked cookies might trigger a desire to eat, even if you weren't hungry before. The scent acts as a sensory trigger, bringing back memories of comfort or pleasure associated with eating cookies. This trigger can lead to the automatic behavior of reaching for a treat, reinforcing the ghost habit over time.

Similarly, certain sounds, like the opening notes of a favorite song, might trigger the urge to dance or sing along, even if you weren't planning to. The auditory trigger activates a memory or emotional response that prompts the behavior. In this way, sensory triggers can lead to the formation of ghost habits that are tied to specific sensory experiences.

- *Internal Dialogue and Beliefs*

Our internal dialogue—the thoughts and beliefs we hold about ourselves and the world—can also act as triggers for ghost habits. These mental triggers are often deeply ingrained and can influence our behavior in subtle ways.

For example, someone who believes that they are not good enough may have an internal dialogue that constantly reinforces this belief. This negative self-talk can trigger ghost habits like avoiding challenges, procrastinating, or engaging in self-sabotaging behaviors. The belief becomes a trigger for behaviors that are designed to protect the person from failure or rejection, even though they ultimately reinforce the very belief they are trying to escape.

Another example is the internal dialogue around success and achievement. Someone who believes that they must always be productive may develop ghost habits of overworking or never allowing themselves to rest. The belief that they must always be doing something becomes a trigger for constant activity, even when rest or relaxation would be more beneficial.

- *Past Experiences and Trauma*

Past experiences, particularly those that are traumatic or emotionally charged, can leave lasting imprints on the subconscious mind, acting as powerful triggers for ghost habits. These events can leave lasting impressions, shaping behavior patterns that persist well beyond the initial experience.

For example, someone who experienced a difficult breakup might develop a ghost habit of avoiding romantic relationships. The pain and emotional turmoil of the past experience become a trigger that prompts the behavior of avoidance, even when the person consciously desires a new relationship. The past experience acts as a subconscious trigger that influences their current behavior, often without their full awareness.

Similarly, someone who has experienced trauma may develop ghost habits as coping mechanisms. For instance, a person who has been through a traumatic event might develop a habit of hypervigilance, constantly scanning their environment for potential threats. This behavior is triggered by the memory of the trauma, even in situations where there is no actual danger. The past experience serves as a powerful trigger that shapes the person's behavior in the present.

- *Physical States*

Our physical state—whether we are tired, hungry, in pain, or feeling energetic—can also act as a trigger for certain behaviors. These triggers are closely linked to the body's need to maintain balance and comfort, and they can lead to the formation of ghost habits.

For example, someone who experiences frequent headaches may develop a ghost habit of reaching for pain medication at the first sign of discomfort. The physical sensation of pain becomes a trigger for the behavior of taking medication, even if the headache is mild and might resolve on its own. This habit can become automatic, with the person responding to the physical trigger without considering alternative ways to manage the pain.

Similarly, hunger is a powerful physical trigger that can lead to the formation of ghost habits around eating. Someone who experiences frequent hunger pangs might develop a habit of snacking throughout the day, even when full meals are available. The physical sensation of hunger becomes a trigger for eating, leading to a routine that can be difficult to break.

Managing and Overcoming Common Triggers

Identifying and understanding common triggers is the first step in managing and overcoming ghost habits. Once you recognize the triggers that influence your behavior, you can begin to take steps to address them and create new, healthier habits.

A powerful approach is to adjust your surroundings in a way that minimizes contact with potential triggers. By altering the environment, you can significantly decrease the chances of encountering situations or stimuli that may lead to undesirable behaviors.. For instance, if you know that certain places or objects trigger unhealthy behaviors, try to remove or change them. This might involve rearranging your home to eliminate visual cues that prompt snacking or finding new social activities that don't revolve around drinking.

Another approach is to develop alternative responses to triggers. For example, if stress is a trigger for smoking, you might practice deep breathing or take a walk whenever you feel stressed. Over time, these new behaviors can become habits themselves, replacing the old ones.

Mindfulness and self-awareness are also key to managing triggers. By staying present and aware of your thoughts, emotions, and behaviors, you can catch yourself before you automatically respond to a trigger. This gives you the opportunity to choose a different, more intentional response.

Conclusion

Common triggers, whether they are environmental cues, emotional states, social norms, routines, sensory experiences, internal dialogue, past experiences, or physical states, play a significant role in the formation and maintenance of ghost habits. Understanding these triggers is essential for gaining control over your behavior and making positive changes in your life. By identifying the triggers that influence your habits, you can take proactive steps to manage them, break free from automatic responses, and create a more intentional and fulfilling life. The journey of recognizing and overcoming common triggers is a powerful step toward greater self-awareness, personal growth, and lasting change.

Techniques to Uncover Triggers

Subconscious triggers play a significant role in shaping our behaviors, often influencing our actions without our conscious awareness. These triggers can be deeply embedded, making them difficult to identify and address. However, by employing specific techniques, we can bring these triggers to the surface, allowing us to understand and modify the behaviors they influence. Here, we explore several effective methods for uncovering subconscious triggers, including journaling, mindfulness, and reflection.

1. Journaling: Writing Your Way to Awareness
Journaling is one of the most powerful tools for uncovering subconscious triggers. By regularly recording your thoughts,

feelings, and experiences, you create a detailed record of your inner world. This process allows you to observe patterns and identify the underlying triggers that may be influencing your behavior.

How to Start Journaling for Trigger Identification:

- Daily Entries: Begin by committing to writing in your journal every day. It doesn't have to be a lengthy process—a few minutes each day can suffice. Focus on documenting your experiences, particularly noting any strong emotions or significant events that occurred.

- Detail Your Reactions: Pay special attention to moments when you felt a strong emotional reaction or engaged in a habitual behavior. For instance, if you found yourself overeating or feeling anxious, describe what was happening around you at the time, how you felt, and what thoughts were running through your mind.

- Look for Patterns: After a few weeks of journaling, review your entries. Look for patterns in your behavior and emotions. You might notice that certain situations, people, or even specific times of day trigger particular responses. For example, you might discover that you tend to feel stressed and reach for a snack every afternoon when work pressure peaks. This pattern indicates a potential subconscious trigger related to stress and food.

- Ask Probing Questions: To delve deeper, ask yourself questions in your journal. Why do I feel this way? What was I thinking right before this behavior occurred? How did the environment or my interactions influence my reaction? These questions can help you dig beneath the surface and bring subconscious triggers to light.

Benefits of Journaling:

- Increased Self-Awareness: Journaling helps you become more attuned to your thoughts and emotions, making it easier to recognize the triggers that drive your behaviors.

- Clearer Understanding: By documenting your experiences, you can see the connections between your triggers and actions more clearly, which can lead to better decision-making and behavior modification.

- Emotional Release: Writing can be a therapeutic way to process emotions, reducing the impact of negative triggers.

2. Mindfulness: Observing Without Judgment

Mindfulness is the practice of paying attention to the present moment with a non-judgmental awareness. This technique is particularly effective for uncovering subconscious triggers because it encourages you to observe your thoughts, feelings, and behaviors as they arise, rather than reacting to them automatically.

How to Practice Mindfulness for Trigger Identification:

- Start with Breath Awareness: Begin your mindfulness practice by focusing on your breath. Feel the gentle flow of air as it moves in and out of your body. This simple act of paying attention can help ground you in the present moment, making it easier to observe your thoughts and feelings.

- Observe Without Reacting: As you become more comfortable with breath awareness, start to expand your focus to include your thoughts and emotions. Notice what comes up without trying to change or judge it. For example, if you feel a wave of anxiety, simply acknowledge it: "I'm feeling anxious right now." Avoid the temptation to analyze or suppress the feeling; just observe it.

- Identify the Trigger: As you observe your thoughts and feelings, try to identify what triggered them. Was it something you saw or heard? A memory? A physical sensation? For instance, you might notice that you feel a sense of dread every time you receive an email from a particular colleague. This observation can help you recognize the email as a trigger for anxiety.

- Stay Present: Mindfulness is about staying in the moment, so if you find your mind wandering to the past or future, gently bring it back to the present. This practice helps you stay focused on what's happening now, which is where subconscious triggers often reveal themselves.

- Body Scan: A body scan is a mindfulness practice where you consciously bring your attention to various parts of your body, starting from your toes and gradually moving up to your head. As you focus on each region, take note of any physical sensations, areas of tension, or feelings of discomfort that arise. This practice can help you identify physical triggers that might be linked to your emotional or behavioral responses. For example, you might realize that you always feel tightness in your chest before a meeting, which could be a physical manifestation of stress.

Benefits of Mindfulness:

- Greater Clarity: Mindfulness helps you see your thoughts and behaviors clearly, without the distortions that can come from reacting impulsively or emotionally.

- Stress Reduction: By staying present and observing your thoughts and emotions, you can reduce the impact of stress triggers.

- Enhanced Emotional Regulation: Mindfulness promotes a calm, balanced state of mind, making it easier to manage your reactions to triggers.

3. Reflection: The Power of Looking Back

Reflection involves taking time to think deeply about your experiences, behaviors, and the triggers that influence them. Unlike mindfulness, which focuses on the present moment, reflection encourages you to look back on past events to gain insights into your subconscious triggers.

How to Use Reflection for Trigger Identification:

- Set Aside Time: To truly reflect, it's essential to find a calm, distraction-free environment that allows for deep and focused thinking.. Set aside regular time—such as at the end of the day or week—to reflect on your experiences.

- Recall Specific Events: Start by recalling specific events where you felt a strong emotional response or engaged in a habitual behavior. For example, think about a time when you felt unusually angry or frustrated. What was happening at the time? Who were you with? What were you thinking?

- Analyze the Situation: Once you've identified a specific event, analyze it in detail. Consider asking yourself reflective questions such as: What event or situation prompted my response? Was there something in my environment, a particular thought, or a physical sensation that preceded my behavior? What patterns can I see when I compare this situation to others where I reacted similarly?

- Connect the Dots: As you reflect on multiple events, look for common threads. For example, you might notice that your frustration often arises during interactions with a certain person or in situations where you feel undervalued. This recognition can help you identify the underlying triggers that drive your behavior.

- Write Down Your Insights: Consider combining reflection with journaling. Writing down your reflections can help solidify your insights and make it easier to see patterns over time. For instance, after reflecting on several stressful situations, you might write: "I tend to react strongly when I feel like my opinions aren't being heard. This triggers my frustration and leads to confrontational behavior."

Benefits of Reflection:

- Deeper Understanding: Reflection allows you to explore your thoughts and behaviors in a more structured way, leading to a deeper understanding of your subconscious triggers.

- Improved Decision-Making: By reflecting on past events, you can learn from your experiences and make better decisions in the future.

- Personal Growth: Regular reflection can help you identify areas for personal growth and development, enabling you to make positive changes in your life.

4. Meditation: Delving into the Subconscious

Meditation, similar to mindfulness, involves focusing the mind and observing your thoughts and feelings. However, meditation often goes a step further, encouraging you to explore the deeper layers of your subconscious mind. This practice can be especially effective for uncovering deep-seated triggers that influence your behavior.

How to Use Meditation for Trigger Identification:

- Choose a Quiet Space: Find a quiet, comfortable space where you can meditate without distractions. Find a comfortable spot where you can either sit or lie down with ease

- Focus on Your Breath: Start your meditation by gently directing your attention to your breathing.. Breathe slowly and deeply, allowing yourself to relax and let go of any tension.

- Allow Thoughts to Surface: As you meditate, allow your thoughts to surface naturally. Instead of trying to control or direct them, simply observe what comes up. Pay attention to any recurring thoughts, memories, or emotions.

- Explore the Underlying Feelings: When a particular thought or emotion arises, take time to explore it. Ask yourself: Where is this feeling coming from? What is it connected to? For example, if you find yourself repeatedly thinking about a stressful work situation, delve into the emotions associated with it. Is it fear, frustration, or something else? This exploration can help you identify the trigger behind the emotion.

- Use Visualization: Visualization is a powerful meditation technique that can help you access deeper layers of your subconscious. Imagine yourself in a situation where you typically experience a strong reaction. Visualize the scenario in detail and observe your thoughts and feelings as they arise. This exercise can help you identify the specific triggers that lead to your habitual responses.

Benefits of Meditation:

- Access to Deeper Insights: Meditation allows you to explore the deeper layers of your mind, uncovering triggers that might be hidden beneath the surface.

- Enhanced Emotional Control: By observing your thoughts and emotions in a meditative state, you can develop greater control over your reactions to triggers.

- Improved Mental Clarity: Regular meditation can lead to a clearer, more focused mind, making it easier to recognize and address subconscious triggers.

5. Cognitive Behavioral Techniques: Rewiring Your Reactions

Cognitive Behavioral Therapy (CBT) techniques are specifically crafted to assist individuals in recognizing and transforming negative thought patterns and behaviors. By focusing on the connection between thoughts, emotions, and actions, CBT provides tools to reframe unhelpful thinking and develop healthier, more constructive habits. These techniques can be highly effective for uncovering and addressing subconscious triggers.

How to Use Cognitive Behavioral Techniques for Trigger Identification:

- Identify Negative Thought Patterns: Start by identifying recurring negative thoughts or beliefs that might be linked to your behaviors. For example, if you have a habit of avoiding social situations, you might identify a thought pattern like, "People won't like me."

- Challenge the Thought: Once you've identified a negative thought, challenge it. Ask yourself: Is this thought rational? What evidence do I have that supports or contradicts it? By challenging the thought, you can begin to weaken its influence as a trigger.

- Reframe the Situation: Reframing involves changing the way you think about a situation. For example, instead of thinking, "I'll fail if I try something new," you might reframe it as, "Trying something new is a learning opportunity." This shift in perspective can reduce the power of triggers associated with fear or anxiety.

- Practice New Responses: Once you've identified and challenged a trigger, practice responding to it in a new way. For example, if stress triggers overeating, practice using relaxation techniques or physical activity as an alternative response. Over time, this new behavior can become a habit, replacing the old trigger-response cycle.

Benefits of Cognitive Behavioral Techniques:

- Empowerment: CBT techniques empower you to take control of your thoughts and behaviors, reducing the influence of negative triggers.

- Long-Term Change: By consistently applying CBT techniques, you can create lasting changes in your thought patterns and behaviors, leading to improved well-being.

- Enhanced Self-Awareness: CBT encourages you to examine your thoughts and beliefs closely, leading to greater self-awareness and insight into your triggers.

Conclusion

Uncovering subconscious triggers is a vital step in gaining control over your behavior and making positive changes in your life. Techniques such as journaling, mindfulness, reflection, meditation, and cognitive behavioral techniques offer powerful ways to bring these hidden triggers to the surface. By regularly practicing these methods, you can develop a deeper understanding of the factors that influence your actions, enabling you to make more intentional choices and break free from automatic, unhelpful behaviors. The journey of identifying and addressing subconscious triggers is a transformative process that can lead to greater self-awareness, personal growth, and a more fulfilling life.

Chapter 4: Breaking the Cycle: Baby Steps to Change

The Importance of Small Steps

Why Small Steps Matter in Habit Change

Change is often daunting, particularly when it involves altering deeply ingrained habits. The prospect of transforming one's life can seem overwhelming, leading many to abandon their efforts before they even begin. This is where the concept of taking small, manageable steps comes into play. Small steps are the cornerstone of effective habit change because they make the process less intimidating, more achievable, and sustainable over the long term. Understanding why small steps are so powerful is essential for anyone looking to break the cycle of negative behaviors and establish new, positive habits.

The Psychological Power of Small Wins

One of the key reasons why small steps are so effective is that they capitalize on the psychological power of "small wins." A small win is a modest but significant accomplishment that fosters a sense of advancement and generates positive momentum.. When we accomplish something, even if it's a small task, our brains release dopamine, a neurotransmitter associated with pleasure and reward. This dopamine release reinforces the behavior, making it more likely that we'll continue on the path toward our larger goals.

Small wins also contribute to a positive feedback loop. Each small success boosts our confidence and motivation, encouraging us to take the next step. This incremental approach helps to create a sense of accomplishment, which is crucial for maintaining the motivation needed to persist with habit change over time. When we focus on small, achievable goals, we are more likely to experience success, which in turn makes us feel capable of achieving even more.

For example, if someone is trying to adopt a healthier lifestyle, starting with a small step like drinking one extra glass of water each day can be a powerful motivator. This small change is easy to accomplish and provides an immediate sense of achievement. As this new habit becomes established, the individual can build on it by incorporating additional small steps, such as taking a short walk each day or adding a serving of vegetables to their meals. Each of these small steps reinforces the overall goal of a healthier lifestyle, making the process feel manageable and rewarding.

Reducing Overwhelm and Resistance

Another reason small steps are effective for habit change is that they reduce the feelings of overwhelm and resistance that often accompany major life changes. When faced with a significant goal, it's common to feel anxious or uncertain about where to start. The sheer size of the task can lead to procrastination or avoidance, as it seems too difficult to tackle all at once.

Small steps break down a large goal into bite-sized pieces, making it easier to take action. By focusing on one small step at a time, the task feels less daunting and more achievable. This approach reduces the mental and emotional resistance that can prevent us from making progress. Instead of feeling overwhelmed by the enormity of the goal, we can concentrate on the next immediate action, which feels more manageable.

For instance, someone who wants to write a book might feel overwhelmed by the idea of completing an entire manuscript. However, if they break the goal down into small steps—such as writing 100 words a day—the task becomes much more approachable. By focusing on the small step of writing just 100 words, they can gradually build up their manuscript without feeling the weight of the entire project. This method reduces the likelihood of giving up due to feeling overwhelmed and increases the chances of successfully completing the book.

Building Sustainable Habits

Sustainability is a crucial factor in habit change. Many people start with grand ambitions, only to find that their initial enthusiasm wanes over time. This is often because they attempt to change too much, too quickly, leading to burnout or failure. Small steps, on the other hand, are more sustainable because they are easier to integrate into daily life without causing disruption.

When we try to make drastic changes, our brains can perceive the shift as a threat, triggering resistance. This is because our habits, even the negative ones, provide a sense of stability and predictability. Sudden, significant changes can be jarring, leading to a return to old habits. In contrast, small steps are less likely to be perceived as threatening, allowing us to gradually adjust to new behaviors without triggering resistance.

Small steps also allow for the gradual development of new habits. Habits are formed through repetition, and the more often a behavior is repeated, the more ingrained it becomes. By starting with small steps, we can establish a foundation of consistency, which is essential for habit formation. Over time, as the small step becomes routine, it can be expanded or built upon, leading to more substantial changes that feel natural and sustainable.

For example, someone who wants to start exercising regularly might begin with a small step like doing five minutes of stretching each morning. This small commitment is easy to maintain and helps to establish the habit of regular physical activity. As this habit becomes ingrained, the individual can gradually increase the duration and intensity of their workouts. Because the change is incremental, it is more likely to be sustainable over the long term.

Overcoming Perfectionism and Fear of Failure

Perfectionism and fear of failure are common obstacles to habit change. Many people set high standards for themselves and feel discouraged if they don't achieve perfection right away. This way of thinking can create hesitation to begin, as the person may fear they won't live up to their own standards. Small steps help to overcome these obstacles by shifting the focus from perfection to progress.

When we take small steps, we give ourselves permission to be imperfect and to learn from the process. Each small step is an opportunity to experiment, make mistakes, and adjust as needed. This approach fosters a growth mindset, where the emphasis is on learning and improvement rather than on immediate success. By reducing the pressure to be perfect, small steps make it easier to take action and maintain momentum.

Moreover, small steps minimize the impact of setbacks. If we set a small, manageable goal and fall short, the consequences are less severe than if we had aimed for a larger, more ambitious goal. This reduces the fear of failure and makes it easier to recover and continue making progress. For instance, if someone's goal is to run a marathon but they miss a training day, it can feel like a major setback. However, if their goal is simply to run for five minutes each day, missing one day feels less significant and easier to bounce back from.

Creating Lasting Change Through Incremental Progress

One of the most compelling reasons to embrace small steps in habit change is that they lead to lasting transformation. While drastic changes can produce quick results, they are often difficult to sustain. In contrast, small, consistent changes build a solid foundation for long-term success.

Incremental progress allows us to adapt to new behaviors gradually, making them more likely to stick. Each small step reinforces the previous one, creating a cumulative effect that leads to significant change over time. This process is often referred to as "compounding," where small, consistent efforts accumulate to produce substantial results.

For example, consider the process of learning a new language. If someone tries to learn an entire language in a few weeks, they may quickly become overwhelmed and give up. However, if they commit to learning just one new word each day, they will have learned over 300 words by the end of the year. While the daily effort may seem small, the cumulative effect is significant and leads to meaningful progress.

The Role of Patience and Persistence

Patience and persistence are essential qualities when taking small steps toward habit change. Because small steps may not produce immediate, dramatic results, it's important to maintain a long-term perspective and trust the process. Patience allows us to stay committed to our goals, even when progress feels slow or incremental.

Consistency is crucial because altering habits is often a non-linear journey. There will be ups and downs, setbacks, and challenges along the way. By taking small steps, we build the resilience needed to keep going, even when things don't go as planned. Each small step is a reminder that progress is being made, no matter how slow it may seem.

Applying Small Steps to Different Areas of Life

The principle of taking small steps can be applied to various areas of life, including health, career, relationships, and personal development. In each of these areas, small, manageable steps can lead to significant improvements over time.

- Health: Instead of overhauling your entire diet, start by adding one extra serving of vegetables to your meals each day. Gradually increase your physical activity by taking short walks or incorporating simple exercises into your routine.

- Career: If you're looking to advance in your career, begin by setting small, achievable goals, such as learning a new skill or networking with one new person each week. Over time, these small actions can lead to new opportunities and career growth.

- Relationships: Strengthen your relationships by making small gestures of appreciation or spending a few extra minutes each day connecting with loved ones. These small actions can build stronger bonds over time.

- Personal Development: Focus on small, daily practices that contribute to your personal growth, such as reading for 10 minutes a day, practicing gratitude, or meditating. These small steps can lead to significant personal transformation over time.

Conclusion

The importance of small steps in habit change cannot be overstated. By focusing on manageable, incremental actions, we reduce feelings of overwhelm, build sustainable habits, overcome perfectionism, and create lasting change. Small steps capitalize on the psychological power of small wins, providing the motivation and momentum needed to persist in the face of challenges. Whether applied to health, career, relationships, or personal development, small steps offer a practical and effective approach to breaking the cycle of negative behaviors and achieving meaningful, long-term change.

Strategies for Baby Steps

When it comes to breaking down ghost habits—those deeply ingrained, often subconscious behaviors that subtly influence our daily lives—starting with small, manageable steps is crucial. By focusing on practical strategies like micro-goals, habit stacking, and reward systems, we can gradually dismantle these habits and replace them with more intentional and positive behaviors.

Here's how you can effectively put these strategies into action.

1. Micro-Goals: Breaking Down the Big Picture

Micro-goals are small, specific, and actionable steps that contribute to a larger goal. They are the building blocks of change, making seemingly overwhelming tasks feel more manageable. The idea behind micro-goals is to focus on the immediate, achievable actions that move you toward your overall objective.

How to Set Effective Micro-Goals:

- Start Small: Begin by identifying a large goal or habit you want to change and break it down into the smallest possible steps. For instance, if your goal is to exercise regularly, a micro-goal might be to start with just five minutes of stretching each morning. This small step is easy to achieve and doesn't require a significant time commitment, making it more likely that you'll stick with it.

- Be Specific: Vague goals like "eat healthier" or "get fit" are difficult to achieve because they lack clarity. Instead, make your micro-goals specific and actionable, such as "replace sugary snacks with fruit" or "take the stairs instead of the elevator at work." Specific goals provide clear direction and make it easier to measure progress.

- Focus on One Goal at a Time: Trying to change multiple habits at once can be overwhelming and lead to burnout. Focus on one micro-goal at a time until it becomes a habit, then move on to the next.

For example, once you've established a routine of drinking a glass of water every morning, you can add another micro-goal, such as going for a 10-minute walk after lunch.

- Celebrate Small Wins: Each time you achieve a micro-goal, take a moment to acknowledge your success. This positive reinforcement helps build momentum and encourages you to continue making progress. Celebrating small wins can be as simple as giving yourself a mental pat on the back or treating yourself to something enjoyable, like a relaxing activity or a favorite snack.

Benefits of Micro-Goals:

- Manageability: Micro-goals are easy to achieve, reducing the risk of feeling overwhelmed and increasing the likelihood of success.

- Motivation: Achieving micro-goals provides a sense of accomplishment, which boosts motivation and confidence.

- Consistency: Small, consistent actions lead to long-term change by gradually replacing old habits with new ones.

2. Habit Stacking: Building on Existing Routines

Habit stacking is an effective technique where you attach a new habit to one you already practice regularly. By doing this, the new behavior becomes seamlessly integrated into your daily routine, making it easier to establish and maintain. By "stacking" the new habit onto an established routine, you can take advantage of the momentum and structure of your current habits to support the formation of new ones.

How to Use Habit Stacking:

- Identify an Existing Habit: Start by identifying a habit that you already perform consistently every day. This could be something as simple as brushing your teeth, making your morning coffee, or checking your email.

- Choose a New Habit to Stack: Next, choose a new habit that you want to develop and "stack" it onto the existing habit. For example, if you want to start meditating, you might decide to meditate for five minutes immediately after brushing your teeth in the morning. The existing habit of brushing your teeth serves as a cue to remind you to meditate.

- Be Consistent: Consistency is key to making habit stacking work. By linking the new habit to an established routine, you create a reliable cue that prompts the desired behavior. With consistent practice, the new habit will gradually become as ingrained and natural as the one it replaced.

- Start Small: Just like with micro-goals, it's important to start with small, manageable habits when using habit stacking. Trying to add a complex or time-consuming habit to your routine can be overwhelming and may lead to failure. Instead, begin with something simple and gradually increase the complexity or duration as the habit becomes more ingrained.

- Use Positive Reinforcement: To reinforce the new habit, use positive reinforcement immediately after completing it. This could be a mental affirmation, a small reward, or simply acknowledging your progress. Incorporating positive reinforcement into your routine can significantly enhance the connection between a new habit and your established behaviors, increasing the likelihood that the habit will become a lasting part of your daily life.

Examples of Habit Stacking:

- Morning Routine: After making your bed (existing habit), take five minutes to stretch (new habit).

- Work Routine: After sending your daily report (existing habit), spend two minutes organizing your desk (new habit).

- Evening Routine: After setting your alarm for the next day (existing habit), write down three things you're grateful for (new habit).

Benefits of Habit Stacking:

- Efficiency: Habit stacking leverages existing routines, making it easier to incorporate new habits without disrupting your daily life.

- Reliability: The consistency of existing habits provides a stable foundation for developing new behaviors.

- Ease of Implementation: By linking new habits to established ones, habit stacking simplifies the process of behavior change.

3. Reward Systems: Reinforcing Positive Behavior

Reward systems are a powerful tool for reinforcing positive behavior and encouraging the formation of new habits. By associating a new habit with a reward, you create a positive feedback loop that makes the habit more enjoyable and increases the likelihood that you'll stick with it.

How to Create an Effective Reward System:

- Choose Meaningful Rewards: The reward should be something that you genuinely enjoy and look forward to. It could be something small, like enjoying a piece of chocolate after completing a workout, or something more substantial, like treating yourself to a spa day after a month of consistent progress. The essential step is to select a reward that resonates deeply with you and provides genuine motivation.

- Make Rewards Immediate: To be effective, rewards should be given immediately after completing the desired behavior. This immediacy helps strengthen the association between the behavior and the reward, making it more likely that the habit will stick. For example, if your goal is to read more, reward yourself with a few minutes of a favorite TV show or a cup of tea right after finishing a reading session.

- Use a Tiered Reward System: For more complex or long-term goals, consider using a tiered reward system where you set up small, medium, and large rewards based on different levels of achievement. For instance, you might reward yourself with a small treat after each successful workout, a new piece of workout gear after a month of consistent exercise, and a weekend getaway after reaching a major fitness milestone.

- Incorporate Social Rewards: Social rewards, such as positive feedback or recognition from others, can also be powerful motivators. Share your progress with friends or family members who can offer encouragement and celebrate your achievements with you. Social rewards tap into our natural desire for connection and approval, making them a valuable addition to your reward system.

- Avoid Overindulgence: While rewards are important, it's also crucial to avoid overindulgence, which can undermine your progress. Ensure that your rewards are proportional to the effort and achievement involved. For example, if your goal is to eat healthier, rewarding yourself with unhealthy food after each healthy meal could be counterproductive. Instead, choose non-food rewards or healthy treats that align with your goals.

Benefits of Reward Systems:

- Increased Motivation: Rewards provide an immediate incentive to engage in positive behaviors, making it easier to stay motivated.

- Positive Reinforcement: By rewarding yourself for good behavior, you strengthen the association between the habit and positive outcomes, making it more likely to stick.

- Sustained Progress: Reward systems help maintain momentum over the long term by providing ongoing incentives for continued effort.

4. Accountability: Engaging Support Systems

Accountability is another effective strategy for breaking down ghost habits. By involving others in your habit-change journey, you create an additional layer of motivation and support. Knowing that someone else is aware of your goals can increase your commitment and help you stay on track.

How to Build Accountability:

- Find an Accountability Partner: Select a reliable individual whom you trust to serve as your accountability partner. This could be a friend, family member, or colleague who is supportive of your goals. Share your specific goals and the steps you plan to take, and ask them to check in with you regularly to discuss your progress.

- Join a Group: Consider joining a group or community that shares similar goals. For example, if you're trying to quit smoking, joining a support group or an online forum can provide encouragement, share strategies, and offer a sense of camaraderie. Group accountability can be particularly powerful because it creates a collective commitment to change.

- Set Up Regular Check-Ins: Consistently arrange meetings with your accountability partner or group to review your progress, address any obstacles, and celebrate your achievements. These check-ins provide an opportunity to reflect on what's working, adjust your approach if needed, and receive feedback and encouragement.

- Use Public Commitments: Making a public commitment to your goals can also increase accountability. For example, you might announce your goal on social media, where your friends and followers can offer support and hold you accountable. Public commitments tap into the desire to maintain a positive image and not let others down, which can be a strong motivator for sticking to your goals.

Benefits of Accountability:

- Increased Commitment: Knowing that someone else is aware of your goals and progress can increase your commitment to follow through.

- Support and Encouragement: Accountability partners and groups provide valuable support, encouragement, and feedback, making the habit-change process more manageable.

- Enhanced Focus: Regular check-ins and public commitments help you stay focused on your goals and maintain momentum over time.

5. Visualization: Picturing Success

Visualization is a powerful mental strategy where you picture yourself effectively carrying out a specific action or reaching a particular objective. This technique allows you to mentally rehearse success, enhancing your ability to achieve it in reality. This technique can be particularly effective for reinforcing new habits and breaking down ghost habits, as it helps to create a clear mental image of success.

How to Use Visualization for Habit Change:

- Create a Clear Mental Image: Start by closing your eyes and picturing yourself engaging in the new habit you want to develop. Imagine every detail, from the environment to how you feel while performing the habit. For example, if your goal is to practice daily meditation, visualize yourself sitting calmly, breathing deeply, and feeling relaxed and focused.

- Engage All Your Senses: Create a mental image that is as detailed and vibrant as possible, involving all your senses to bring it to life.. Imagine the sounds, smells, and physical sensations associated with the habit. The more detailed and realistic the visualization, the more effective it will be in reinforcing the behavior.

- Visualize the Outcome: In addition to visualizing the behavior itself, imagine the positive outcomes that will result from it. For example, if your goal is to exercise regularly, visualize yourself feeling energized, strong, and healthy as a result of your workouts. This positive reinforcement can help motivate you to take action.

- Practice Regularly: Make visualization a regular part of your routine, ideally practicing it daily. Consistent visualization helps to reinforce the desired behavior in your mind, making it more likely that you'll follow through in real life.

Benefits of Visualization:

- Mental Rehearsal: Visualization acts as a form of mental rehearsal, preparing your mind and body for the desired behavior.

- Increased Confidence: By repeatedly picturing yourself succeeding, you build confidence in your ability to achieve your goals.

- Enhanced Motivation: Visualization helps you stay focused on the positive outcomes of your efforts, increasing your motivation to persist.

Conclusion

Breaking down ghost habits and creating positive change in your life requires a strategic approach. By employing techniques such as micro-goals, habit stacking, reward systems, accountability, and visualization, you can take small, manageable steps toward your goals. These strategies make the process of habit change more achievable, sustainable, and rewarding, helping you to overcome the barriers that have held you back in the past. Whether you're aiming to improve your health, boost your productivity, or enhance your personal relationships, these practical strategies provide a clear path to success, one step at a time.

Overcoming Setbacks

The Inevitability of Setbacks

Setbacks are an inevitable part of any journey toward change, particularly when it comes to breaking long-established habits and patterns of behavior. These moments of difficulty or regression can feel discouraging, but they are a normal part of the process and should be anticipated rather than feared. Understanding that setbacks are a natural occurrence can help you prepare for them, navigate through them effectively, and continue progressing toward your goals without falling back into denial or giving up entirely.

Why Setbacks Happen

Setbacks occur for various reasons, many of which are beyond our control. They can be triggered by external factors such as stress, unexpected life events, or changes in your environment that make it more challenging to maintain new habits. Internal factors, such as fatigue, emotional upheaval, or a lapse in motivation, can also contribute to setbacks. Understanding the underlying causes of a setback is the essential first step towards overcoming it.

- *Old Habits Die Hard:*

Our brains are wired to favor familiar routines and behaviors because they require less cognitive effort. When you try to replace an old habit with a new one, the brain often defaults to the familiar pattern, especially under stress or when you're not fully focused. This is why you might find yourself slipping back into old behaviors despite your best intentions.

- *Unrealistic Expectations*:

Setting overly ambitious goals can set you up for setbacks. If your expectations are too high, you may become discouraged when you don't see immediate results or when progress is slower than expected. This disappointment can lead to a loss of motivation and a return to old habits.

- *Emotional Triggers:*

Emotions play a significant role in our behavior. Stress, anxiety, sadness, or even boredom can trigger a return to old habits as a way to cope with these emotions. For example, someone who is trying to quit smoking might find themselves reaching for a cigarette during a particularly stressful day.

- *External Pressures:*

Life is full of unexpected events that can disrupt your routine and make it difficult to stick to new habits. A busy period at work, family responsibilities, or social obligations can all contribute to setbacks by reducing the time and energy you have available to focus on your goals.

Navigating Setbacks Without Falling Back into Denial

While setbacks are a natural part of the change process, it's crucial to navigate them effectively to avoid falling back into denial or abandoning your efforts altogether. Here are some strategies for dealing with setbacks and maintaining your progress:

1. *Acknowledge the Setback*

The first and most important step in overcoming a setback is to acknowledge it. Denial only serves to prolong the problem and makes it more difficult to address the underlying issues. Instead of ignoring or downplaying the setback, take a moment to recognize what has happened. Acknowledge the setback without judgment or self-criticism. Understand that setbacks are a normal part of the process and that they don't define your overall progress.

How to Acknowledge a Setback:

- *Be Honest with Yourself:*

Take a moment to pause and consider what didn't go as planned. What triggered the setback? How did you respond? Acknowledge your feelings, whether it's frustration, disappointment, or guilt, but don't dwell on them. Recognizing the setback is the first step in moving forward.

- *Avoid Self-Blame:*

It's easy to fall into the trap of self-blame when things don't go as planned. However, blaming yourself only undermines your confidence and motivation. Instead, view the setback as a learning opportunity and a chance to grow stronger in your resolve.

1. *Analyze the Cause*

Once you've acknowledged the setback, the next step is to analyze the cause. Understanding why the setback occurred can provide valuable insights that will help you prevent similar issues in the future.

Questions to Consider:

- What were the specific circumstances that led to the setback? Was it triggered by stress, fatigue, an unexpected event, or something else?

- Were there warning signs you missed? Did you notice any cues or patterns leading up to the setback that you can be more mindful of in the future?

- What role did your emotions play? Did you experience any emotional triggers that contributed to the setback? How did you handle those emotions?

By analyzing the cause of the setback, you can identify patterns and triggers that may need to be addressed. This understanding allows you to develop strategies for avoiding similar setbacks in the future.

1. *Reframe the Setback as a Learning Opportunity*

Setbacks can be valuable learning experiences if you approach them with the right mindset. Instead of viewing a setback as a failure, reframe it as an opportunity to learn more about yourself and your habits.

How to Reframe a Setback:

- *Focus on the Lessons Learned:*

Consider what valuable lessons you can take away from this setback. What could you do differently next time? How can you use this experience to strengthen your resolve and improve your approach?

- *Celebrate Your Progress:*

Even in the face of a setback, it's important to recognize the progress you've made. Reflect on how far you've come and the positive changes you've already implemented. This perspective can help you maintain motivation and continue moving forward.

1. *Adjust Your Strategy*

After analyzing the cause of the setback and reframing it as a learning opportunity, it's time to adjust your strategy. This might involve making changes to your approach, setting new goals, or finding alternative ways to cope with triggers.

Steps to Adjust Your Strategy:

- *Revisit Your Goals:*

If your original goals were too ambitious or unrealistic, consider breaking them down into smaller, more manageable steps. This makes it easier to stay on track and reduces the likelihood of future setbacks.

- *Develop Coping Mechanisms:*

If emotional triggers played a role in the setback, develop new coping mechanisms to manage these emotions more effectively. This could include stress-relief techniques like deep breathing, exercise, or mindfulness practices.

- *Modify Your Environment:*

If environmental factors contributed to the setback, consider making changes to your environment that support your goals. For example, if certain social situations make it difficult to stick to your new habits, find ways to navigate these situations more effectively or limit your exposure to them.

1. *Recommit to Your Goals*

After adjusting your strategy, it's important to recommit to your goals. Setbacks can sometimes make you question your ability to achieve your goals, but it's essential to renew your commitment and keep moving forward.

How to Recommit:

- *Set a New Start Date:*

Choose a specific date to restart your efforts. This can help you mentally prepare and create a sense of renewed determination.

- *Revisit Your Motivation:*

Reflect on the original reasons and motivations that led you to establish your goals. What benefits will you gain from achieving them? Keep these motivations at the forefront of your mind as you recommit to your goals.

- *Visualize Success:*

Visualization can be a powerful tool for reinforcing your commitment. Take a few moments each day to visualize yourself successfully achieving your goals. Picture how you'll feel, what you'll be doing, and the positive impact it will have on your life.

1. *Seek Support*

You don't have to navigate setbacks alone. Seeking support from others can provide encouragement, accountability, and valuable insights that help you stay on track.

Ways to Seek Support:

- *Talk to a Friend or Family Member:*

Sharing your experience with someone you trust can help you process the setback and gain a new perspective. They can provide motivation, guidance, and a strong emotional foundation.

- *Join a Support Group:*

Consider joining a support group or community of people who share similar goals. Group support can provide a sense of camaraderie and accountability, making it easier to stay motivated.

- *Consult a Professional:*

If you're struggling to overcome setbacks on your own, consider seeking help from a coach, therapist, or counselor. They can provide personalized guidance and strategies to help you navigate challenges and achieve your goals.

1. *Practice Self-Compassion*

Finally, practicing self-compassion is crucial when dealing with setbacks. Being kind to yourself during difficult times helps to reduce negative emotions like guilt and shame, which can otherwise lead to a cycle of denial and further setbacks.

How to Practice Self-Compassion:

- *Acknowledge Your Humanity:*

Understand that setbacks are a normal part of the human experience. Everyone faces challenges and setbacks, and they don't make you any less capable or deserving of success.

- *Speak to Yourself Kindly:*

Pay attention to your inner dialogue and replace self-criticism with supportive, encouraging words. Rather than telling yourself, "I failed once more," consider saying, "This is just a hurdle," but it's an opportunity to learn and move forward.

- *Treat Yourself with Care:*

Engage in activities that promote self-care and well-being. This might include spending time with loved ones, engaging in hobbies, or practicing relaxation techniques. Taking care of yourself physically, emotionally, and mentally helps build resilience and prepares you to bounce back from setbacks.

Conclusion

Setbacks are an inevitable part of the journey toward breaking old habits and establishing new ones. While they can be challenging, setbacks also offer valuable opportunities for growth and learning. By acknowledging setbacks, analyzing their causes, reframing them as learning experiences, and adjusting your strategy, you can navigate these challenges without falling back into denial. Recommitting to your goals, seeking support, and practicing self-compassion are essential steps in overcoming setbacks and continuing on the path to positive change. Remember, setbacks do not define your journey; they are simply part of the process, and with the right approach, you can overcome them and achieve lasting   transformation.

Chapter 5: Sustaining Change and Building New Habits

Creating Sustainable Habits

Understanding Ghost Habits and the Need for Positive Change

Ghost habits are those subconscious, automatic behaviors that we often engage in without even realizing it. These habits are typically formed over time through repetition and have become so ingrained in our daily lives that they operate below the level of conscious awareness. While some ghost habits may be harmless or even beneficial, others can be detrimental to our well-being, productivity, or relationships. To create a more fulfilling and intentional life, it's essential to identify these ghost habits and replace them with positive, conscious habits that align with our values and goals.

- **The Process of Replacing Ghost Habits**

Replacing ghost habits with positive habits is a process that requires awareness, intentionality, and consistency. This transformation doesn't happen overnight, but with the right strategies, it is entirely achievable. The following steps outline a practical approach to replacing ghost habits with new, sustainable behaviors.

1. *Awareness: Identifying Ghost Habits*

The first step in replacing ghost habits is becoming aware of them. Since these habits are often subconscious, bringing them into conscious awareness is crucial. Without this awareness, it's impossible to change what you don't recognize.

How to Identify Ghost Habits:

- *Mindful Observation:*

Pay attention to your daily routines and behaviors. Observe any actions you perform on autopilot, without conscious thought. These might include habits like checking your phone as soon as you wake up, snacking when you're not hungry, or responding to stress with negative self-talk.

- *Journaling:*

Keep a journal where you document your behaviors, thoughts, and emotions throughout the day. Look for patterns that indicate the presence of ghost habits. For example, do you always reach for a sugary snack in the afternoon? Do you frequently procrastinate on certain tasks? These patterns can reveal habits that operate subconsciously.

- *Seek Feedback:*

Sometimes, it's challenging to identify your ghost habits on your own. Ask trusted friends, family members, or colleagues if they've noticed any behaviors that you seem to engage in automatically. They might offer insights into habits that you weren't aware of.

1. *Set Clear, Positive Goals*

Once you've identified the ghost habits you want to change, the next step is to set clear, positive goals for the new habits you want to establish. It's essential to focus on what you want to achieve rather than just what you want to eliminate. Positive goals are more motivating and provide a clear direction for change.

How to Set Effective Goals:

- *Be Specific:*

Instead of setting a vague goal like "stop snacking," create a specific goal such as "eat a piece of fruit as a mid-afternoon snack." Specific goals make it easier to take concrete action and measure your progress.

- *Focus on the Positive:*

Frame your goals in a positive light. For example, rather than saying, "I want to stop procrastinating," you could say, "I want to complete one task each day without delay." Reframing your perspective in a positive light directs your attention away from what you want to steer clear of and instead emphasizes the goals you aim to accomplish.

- *Align with Your Values:*

Make sure that your goals are in harmony with your fundamental beliefs and align with your long-term vision for the future. When your goals are connected to your values, you're more likely to stay committed to them. For instance, if health is a core value, setting a goal to incorporate more physical activity into your daily routine will feel more meaningful and motivating.

1. *Replace Old Cues with New Ones*

Ghost habits are often triggered by specific cues in your environment or emotions. To replace these habits with new ones, it's essential to identify these cues and replace them with new, positive triggers that prompt the desired behavior.

How to Replace Old Cues:

- *Identify Triggers:*

Start by identifying the cues that trigger your ghost habits. These could be specific times of day, locations, emotional states, or even particular people. For example, if you tend to snack mindlessly in the evening, the trigger might be sitting down in front of the TV after dinner.

- *Introduce New Triggers:*

Once you've identified the triggers, introduce new, positive cues that align with the habit you want to establish. For example, if your goal is to exercise more, you might place your workout clothes next to your bed as a reminder to exercise first thing in the morning. Or, if you want to practice mindfulness, you could set a reminder on your phone to take a few deep breaths every hour.

- *Change Your Environment:*

Sometimes, altering your environment can help you break free from old habits and establish new ones. For instance, if you want to reduce your sugar intake, remove sugary snacks from your home and replace them with healthier options like fruits and nuts. By making these changes, you create a new environment that supports your goals.

1. Start Small and Build Consistency

One of the most effective ways to replace ghost habits is to start small and build consistency over time. Small, manageable steps are easier to sustain and can lead to significant change when practiced consistently.

How to Start Small:

- *Micro-Habits:*

Begin with micro-habits, which are tiny, easily achievable actions that require minimal effort. For example, if you want to start meditating, begin with just one minute of meditation each day. As you establish this routine, begin to slowly extend the length of time you dedicate to it.

- *Habit Stacking:*

Habit stacking is a strategy where you connect a new behavior to an already established routine. This method leverages the stability of your current habits to make it easier to integrate the new one into your daily life. For example, if you already brush your teeth every morning, you could stack a new habit of doing five push-ups right after brushing your teeth. This technique leverages the consistency of your existing habits to help establish new ones.

- *Celebrate Small Wins:*

Every time you successfully perform your new habit, celebrate your progress. This could be as simple as acknowledging your success or rewarding yourself with something small and enjoyable. Celebrating small wins reinforces positive behavior and helps build momentum.

1. *Use Positive Reinforcement*

Positive reinforcement is a powerful tool for establishing new habits. By rewarding yourself for engaging in the desired behavior, you strengthen the association between the habit and positive outcomes, making it more likely to stick.

How to Use Positive Reinforcement:

- *Immediate Rewards:*

Provide yourself with immediate rewards after completing the desired behavior. For example, if your goal is to exercise daily, treat yourself to a relaxing bath or a favorite healthy snack after each workout. The immediate reward creates a positive feedback loop that encourages repetition.

- *Progressive Rewards:*

As you maintain consistency with your new habit, introduce progressive rewards for reaching specific milestones. For instance, after maintaining a week of steady progress, you could treat yourself to a relaxing movie night as a reward. After a month, you might treat yourself to a new book or a special outing. Progressive rewards keep you motivated and engaged in the long-term process of habit formation.

- *Social Rewards:*

Keep your loved ones, close friends, or a supportive community in the loop about your progress. Positive feedback and encouragement from others can serve as a powerful form of reinforcement. Social rewards tap into our natural desire for connection and validation, making it easier to stay motivated.

1. *Reframe Setbacks as Learning Opportunities*

Setbacks are a natural part of the habit-change process, but they don't have to derail your progress. Instead of viewing setbacks as failures, reframe them as learning opportunities that can help you improve your approach.

How to Reframe Setbacks:

- *Analyze the Setback:*

When a setback occurs, take time to analyze what happened. What triggered the old habit? How did you respond? What could you do differently next time?

By understanding the cause of the setback, you can develop strategies to prevent it from happening again.

- *Adjust Your Strategy:*

Use the insights gained from analyzing the setback to adjust your approach. This might involve modifying your goals, changing your environment, or introducing new rewards or support systems.

- *Stay Positive:*

Remember that setbacks are a normal part of the process and don't define your overall progress. Stay focused on your long-term goals and remind yourself of the positive changes you've already made.

1. *Make It a Lifestyle, Not a Goal*

To ensure that your new habits are sustainable, it's essential to integrate them into your lifestyle rather than viewing them as temporary goals. When a habit becomes part of your identity and daily routine, it's more likely to stick for the long term.

How to Integrate New Habits into Your Lifestyle:

- *Consistency:*

To successfully integrate a habit into your daily routine, consistency is essential. Strive to engage in your new habit at a consistent time or within the same context every day. The more consistent you are, the more automatic the habit will become.

- *Identity Shift:*

Begin to identify yourself with the new habit. For example, if your goal is to start running regularly, start thinking of yourself as a runner. This identity shift helps reinforce the habit and makes it feel like a natural part of who you are.

- *Continuous Improvement:*

Even after a habit becomes established, continue looking for ways to improve and refine it. This might involve setting new challenges, learning more about the behavior, or finding new ways to enjoy it. Continuous improvement keeps the habit fresh and engaging, reducing the risk of regression.

1. *Seek Support and Accountability*

Having a support system can make a significant difference in your ability to sustain new habits. Whether it's a friend, family member, or online community, support and accountability help keep you motivated and on track.

How to Build a Support System:

- *Accountability Partner:*

Seek out an accountability partner who either shares similar goals or is committed to supporting you in your journey. Check in with each other regularly to discuss progress, challenges, and successes. Knowing that someone else is aware of your goals can increase your commitment and help you stay focused.

- *Join a Group:*

Explore the benefits of becoming part of a community or group that aligns with your aspirations. This could be a fitness class, a book club, or an online forum. Group support provides a sense of camaraderie and shared purpose, making it easier to stay motivated.

- *Share Your Goals:*

Don't be afraid to share your goals with others. Whether it's through social media, a blog, or casual conversations, sharing your progress and challenges can help reinforce your commitment and inspire others.

Conclusion

Creating sustainable habits involves more than just breaking old patterns; it requires a thoughtful and intentional approach that incorporates awareness, goal-setting, environmental changes, consistency, and positive reinforcement. By identifying ghost habits and replacing them with positive, conscious behaviors, you can build a more fulfilling and intentional life. Keep in mind that progress is a gradual process, and experiencing setbacks along the way is completely normal. By staying committed, seeking support, and making your new habits an integral part of your lifestyle, you can achieve lasting transformation and continue growing toward your fullest potential.

Building a Support System

The Importance of Support in Habit Change

Sustaining habit change is a challenging process that requires more than just personal determination and willpower. While internal motivation is crucial, the role of external support is equally important in ensuring long-term success. Building a robust support system that includes accountability, community, and encouragement can make the difference between short-lived attempts and lasting transformation. This chapter explores how these elements work together to create an environment conducive to sustained habit change.

Accountability: The Power of Being Answerable

Accountability is one of the most effective tools in sustaining habit change. When you're accountable to someone else, whether it's a friend, a mentor, or a group, you're more likely to stay committed to your goals. Accountability creates a sense of responsibility and helps to keep you on track, even when your internal motivation wanes.

How Accountability Works:

- *External Motivation:*

Being accountable to someone else provides an external source of motivation. Knowing that someone else is aware of your goals and progress can push you to follow through, even on days when you might otherwise skip a workout, indulge in a bad habit, or procrastinate on a task.

- *Regular Check-Ins:*

Accountability often involves regular check-ins where you report your progress, discuss challenges, and set new goals. These check-ins can be formal or informal, depending on your arrangement. The key is to establish a routine that keeps you focused and engaged.

- *Constructive Feedback:*

Accountability partners can offer constructive feedback that helps you refine your approach and overcome obstacles. They can provide a different perspective, suggest new strategies, or simply offer encouragement when you're feeling discouraged.

Types of Accountability:

- *One-on-One Accountability:*

This involves partnering with someone who shares your goals or is supportive of your efforts. You might choose a friend, family member, or colleague who is willing to check in with you regularly and hold you accountable for your actions. This type of accountability is personalized and can be tailored to your specific needs and preferences.

- *Group Accountability:*

Becoming part of a community where individuals share similar aspirations can greatly enhance your sense of accountability. Whether it's a fitness class, a book club, or a professional development group, being part of a community with shared objectives creates a collective sense of responsibility. Group accountability can be particularly effective because it leverages the social pressure and support of the group to keep each member on track.

- *Professional Accountability:*

Hiring a coach, therapist, or mentor can provide a structured form of accountability. Professionals offer expertise, guidance, and regular check-ins to help you achieve your goals. This type of accountability is especially useful if you're working on complex or long-term goals that require specialized knowledge and support.

Building Accountability into Your Routine:

- *Set Clear Expectations:*

When establishing an accountability relationship, be clear about your goals, the frequency of check-ins, and the type of feedback you're looking for. This clarity ensures that both you and your accountability partner are on the same page.

- *Be Consistent:*

Consistency is key to effective accountability. Whether you're meeting with a group, checking in with a partner, or working with a coach, stick to a regular schedule. Consistent accountability helps to reinforce your commitment and keeps your goals top of mind.

- *Track Progress:*

Use tools like journals, apps, or spreadsheets to track your progress and share it with your accountability partner. Tracking progress provides tangible evidence of your achievements and highlights areas where you might need to adjust your approach.

Community: The Strength of Collective Support

Community plays a vital role in sustaining habit change by providing a sense of belonging, shared purpose, and mutual support. Being part of a community with similar goals can amplify your motivation, inspire you to keep going, and offer a safety net during challenging times.

The Role of Community in Habit Change:

- *Shared Experiences:*

Being part of a community allows you to connect with others who are on the same journey. Sharing experiences, challenges, and successes with like-minded individuals creates a sense of camaraderie and reduces the feeling of isolation that can sometimes accompany habit change.

- *Encouragement and Support:*

Communities provide ongoing encouragement and support, which can be crucial during difficult periods. When you're struggling with a setback or feeling unmotivated, the collective strength of the community can lift you up and help you regain your focus.

- *Diverse Perspectives:*

A community offers a range of perspectives, ideas, and strategies for overcoming obstacles. By engaging with others who have different experiences and insights, you can learn new approaches to habit change that you might not have considered on your own.

- *Accountability Within the Group:*

Community-based accountability is another powerful aspect of being part of a group. When you're part of a community, you naturally feel a sense of responsibility to contribute and stay committed to your goals, knowing that others are counting on you.

Finding and Building Your Community:

- *Join Existing Groups:*

Look for existing groups or communities that align with your goals. Consider joining a nearby club, participating in an online forum, or engaging with a social media community. Joining an established community gives you immediate access to a network of people who share your interests and objectives.

- *Create Your Own Group:*

If you can't find a community that fits your needs, consider creating your own. Invite friends, family members, or colleagues who have similar goals to join you in forming a group. This could be as simple as starting a weekly accountability call or creating a private online group where you share progress and support each other.

- *Participate Actively:*

Being an active participant in your community is key to reaping the benefits of collective support. Attend meetings, engage in discussions, offer help to others, and share your own experiences. The more you contribute, the more you'll feel connected and supported by the group.

Support: Encouragement and Guidance on the Journey

Support, whether emotional, practical, or informational, is essential for sustaining habit change. Having a support system means you don't have to navigate the challenges of change alone; you have people who believe in you, offer guidance, and help you stay focused on your goals.

Types of Support:

- *Emotional Support:*

Emotional support involves having someone who listens to you, empathizes with your struggles, and encourages you during difficult times. This type of support helps you manage the emotional ups and downs that come with habit change and reinforces your belief in your ability to succeed.

- *Practical Support:*

Practical support includes tangible assistance, such as helping you develop a plan, providing resources, or assisting with tasks that make it easier to stick to your goals. For example, a friend might help you meal prep for the week if you're trying to eat healthier, or a partner might take on extra household responsibilities to free up time for your new exercise routine.

- *Informational Support:*

Informational support involves providing knowledge, advice, or feedback that helps you navigate the challenges of habit change. This could come from a mentor who shares their expertise, a coach who offers guidance, or a community that shares tips and strategies. Informational support helps you make informed decisions and avoid common pitfalls.

Building a Strong Support System:

- *Identify Your Needs:*

Start by identifying the types of support you need most. Do you need emotional encouragement, practical assistance, or informational guidance? Understanding your needs will help you seek out the right people and resources to support you.

- *Seek Out Supportive People:*

Surround yourself with people who are positive, encouraging, and invested in your success. This might include friends, family members, colleagues, or professionals who can offer the support you need. Be open to asking for help and letting others know how they can support you.

Effectively articulate your objectives and requirements to your support network. Share your aspirations with them and clearly outline the ways in which they can assist you in reaching your goals. Clear communication ensures that everyone is on the same page and can provide the support you need in the most effective way.

- *Reciprocate Support:*

Support is a two-way street. While it's important to receive support, it's equally important to offer it in return. Be there for others in your support system, offering encouragement, advice, or assistance when they need it. This mutual exchange strengthens relationships and fosters a sense of community.

The Synergy of Accountability, Community, and Support

When combined, accountability, community, and support create a powerful synergy that significantly enhances your ability to sustain habit change. Each element reinforces the others, creating a comprehensive support system that addresses the various challenges you might face on your journey.

- Accountability ensures that you stay focused and committed, knowing that others are aware of your goals and progress.

- Being part of a community fosters a deep sense of belonging and shared goals, which can make the process of changing habits more enjoyable and less lonely. Engaging with others who are on a similar path adds meaning to the journey, transforming it from an individual challenge into a collective experience.

- Support offers the emotional, practical, and informational resources you need to overcome obstacles and stay motivated.

Together, these elements create a strong foundation for lasting change. When you're accountable to others, part of a supportive community, and have access to the resources and encouragement you need, you're far more likely to succeed in building new, constructive habits that resonate with your aspirations and core principles..

Conclusion

Building a support system that includes accountability, community, and support is essential for sustaining habit change. These elements work together to provide the motivation, encouragement, and resources you need to overcome challenges and stay committed to your goals. No matter if your goal is to boost your health, climb the career ladder, or grow personally, having a reliable support system can be the key to achieving long-term success. Remember, you don't have to go through the process of habit change alone—by leveraging the power of accountability, community, and support, you can create a positive and empowering environment that fosters growth and transformation.

The Long-Term Impact of Breaking Ghost Habits

Introduction to Ghost Habits and Their Influence

Ghost habits are the subtle, often subconscious routines that have become ingrained in our daily lives, shaping our behaviors, thoughts, and emotions without our conscious awareness. These habits, while sometimes benign, can also be detrimental, quietly undermining our well-being, relationships, and personal growth. The process of identifying and breaking these ghost habits is not just about eliminating negative patterns but also about unlocking the potential for profound, long-term benefits. Overcoming ghost habits can lead to significant improvements in mental health, relationships, and overall personal growth, ultimately allowing us to live more intentional, fulfilling lives.

Improved Mental Health

One of the most significant long-term benefits of breaking ghost habits is the improvement in mental health. Ghost habits, especially those rooted in negative thought patterns or unhealthy coping mechanisms, can contribute to stress, anxiety, and depression. By recognizing and addressing these habits, we can foster a healthier mental state and build resilience against psychological challenges.

Reducing Stress and Anxiety:

- *Breaking the Cycle of Negative Thinking:*

Many ghost habits involve automatic negative thoughts that can fuel stress and anxiety. These thoughts might include self-criticism, catastrophizing, or assuming the worst in situations. By becoming aware of these patterns and actively working to replace them with more positive, balanced thinking, we can reduce the frequency and intensity of stress and anxiety. This shift not only alleviates immediate discomfort but also builds long-term emotional resilience.

- *Adopting Healthier Coping Mechanisms:*

Unseen or unconscious habits frequently manifest as harmful coping strategies, such as turning to food for comfort, overindulging in alcohol, or engaging in avoidance tactics to escape from stress or emotional pain. These habits may provide temporary relief but ultimately exacerbate stress and anxiety. By replacing these habits with healthier alternatives—such as exercise, meditation, or seeking social support—we can manage stress more effectively and create a more stable emotional foundation.

Enhancing Self-Awareness and Emotional Regulation:

- *Increased Self-Awareness:*

Breaking ghost habits requires a heightened level of self-awareness, which is itself a major benefit. As we start to closely observe our actions and the factors that influence them, we begin to uncover a more profound awareness of our emotional patterns and responses. This self-awareness enables us to respond to situations more thoughtfully, rather than reacting impulsively or out of habit.

- *Improved Emotional Regulation:*

With greater awareness comes improved emotional regulation. When we are conscious of our triggers and habitual responses, we can choose how to respond rather than being controlled by our emotions. This ability to regulate our emotions leads to a more balanced and peaceful state of mind, reducing the likelihood of emotional extremes that can harm mental health.

Strengthened Relationships

The impact of ghost habits extends beyond the individual, often influencing our interactions with others. Unaddressed ghost habits can strain relationships, leading to misunderstandings, conflicts, and emotional distance. Conversely, overcoming these habits can significantly enhance the quality of our relationships, fostering deeper connections, improved communication, and greater empathy.

Improved Communication and Understanding:

- *Breaking Patterns of Miscommunication:*

Ghost habits often include patterns of communication that are less than ideal—such as interrupting others, shutting down during disagreements, or avoiding difficult conversations. These habits can create misunderstandings and prevent effective communication. By recognizing and changing these habits, we open the door to clearer, more honest communication. This improvement fosters mutual understanding and reduces the potential for conflict.

- *Cultivating Active Listening:*

One of the positive habits that can replace ghost habits is active listening. By fully engaging with what the other person is saying—without the distractions of our automatic responses or preconceived notions—we show respect and build trust in our relationships. Active listening leads to more meaningful interactions and strengthens the bond between individuals.

Enhanced Empathy and Compassion:

- *Overcoming Self-Centered Habits:*

Ghost habits can sometimes manifest as self-centered behaviors, where we prioritize our own needs and perspectives over those of others. These habits might include dominating conversations, dismissing others' feelings, or being inflexible in our views. By becoming aware of these tendencies and working to replace them with more empathetic behaviors, we can foster greater compassion and understanding in our relationships.

- *Building Emotional Support Networks:*

As we become more empathetic and understanding, we naturally build stronger emotional support networks. These networks are crucial for navigating life's challenges, as they provide a sense of belonging and security. By offering and receiving emotional support, we deepen our connections with others and create a community of mutual care and respect.

Personal Growth and Fulfillment

Breaking ghost habits is a catalyst for personal growth, as it encourages us to live more intentionally and align our behaviors with our values and goals. This process of self-improvement leads to greater fulfillment and a more purposeful life.

Increased Self-Efficacy and Confidence:

- *Mastery Over Habits:*

Successfully overcoming ghost habits instills a sense of mastery and control over our lives. This accomplishment boosts self-efficacy, the belief in our ability to effect change and achieve our goals. As we gain confidence in our capacity to transform our behaviors, we are more likely to take on new challenges and pursue personal growth.

- *Building a Growth Mindset:*

The process of breaking ghost habits often involves embracing a growth mindset—the belief that our abilities and intelligence can be developed through effort and learning. This mindset encourages us to view challenges as opportunities for growth rather than obstacles. As we adopt a growth mindset, we become more resilient in the face of setbacks and more committed to continuous self-improvement.

Alignment with Personal Values and Goals:

- *Living Intentionally:*

Ghost habits can lead us to live on autopilot, where our actions are dictated by routine rather than by conscious choice. By breaking these habits, we create the space to live more intentionally, making decisions that align with our values and long-term goals. This intentionality fosters a deeper sense of purpose and fulfillment, as our actions are guided by what truly matters to us.

- *Pursuing Meaningful Goals:*

As we replace ghost habits with positive, intentional behaviors, we are better equipped to pursue meaningful goals. Whether it's advancing in our careers, building stronger relationships, or contributing to our communities, we approach our goals with greater clarity and determination. This pursuit of meaningful goals leads to a more satisfying and rewarding life.

Greater Resilience and Adaptability:

- *Overcoming Setbacks:*

The journey of breaking ghost habits often involves setbacks and challenges. However, each setback provides an opportunity to learn and grow stronger. As we navigate these challenges, we build resilience—the ability to bounce back from adversity. This resilience not only helps us maintain our progress but also prepares us to handle future challenges with greater confidence and grace.

- *Adapting to Change:*

In today's fast-paced environment, the capacity to adjust and evolve is essential for success.. By breaking ghost habits and cultivating new, positive behaviors, we develop the flexibility needed to adapt to new circumstances. This adaptability allows us to thrive in the face of change, as we are not bound by rigid routines or outdated habits.

Contributing to a Positive Ripple Effect

The benefits of breaking ghost habits extend beyond the individual, creating a positive ripple effect that influences others and the broader community. As we improve our mental health, strengthen our relationships, and grow personally, we contribute to a more positive and supportive environment for those around us.

Influencing Others Positively:

- *Leading by Example:*

When we successfully break ghost habits and replace them with positive behaviors, we set an example for others. Our actions demonstrate the power of intentional living and the potential for change. This influence can inspire others to embark on their own journeys of self-improvement, creating a ripple effect of positive change.

- *Creating a Supportive Environment:*

As we cultivate healthier habits and stronger relationships, we contribute to a more supportive and nurturing environment for those around us. Whether it's at home, at work, or in our communities, our positive influence helps to create spaces where others feel encouraged, valued, and empowered to pursue their goals.

Fostering a Culture of Growth and Well-Being:

- *Promoting Mental Health and Well-Being:*

By prioritizing our mental health and well-being, we contribute to a culture that values these aspects of life. This change in perspective motivates individuals to prioritize their mental well-being and reach out for help when necessary. In turn, this collective emphasis on well-being fosters a healthier, more resilient community.

- *Encouraging Personal Development:*

As we continue to grow and develop, we naturally encourage others to do the same. Whether it's through mentorship, collaboration, or simply sharing our experiences, we contribute to a culture that values personal development and continuous learning. This culture of growth benefits everyone, as it promotes innovation, creativity, and a shared commitment to excellence.

Conclusion

The long-term impact of breaking ghost habits is far-reaching, touching every aspect of our lives—from mental health and relationships to personal growth and broader community well-being. By identifying and overcoming these subconscious patterns, we unlock the potential for profound transformation, leading to a more intentional, fulfilling, and purposeful life. As we continue on this journey, the benefits extend beyond ourselves, creating a positive ripple effect that influences others and contributes to a culture of growth, well-being, and mutual support.

Chapter 6: Case Studies and Personal Stories

Real-Life Examples: Overcoming Ghost Habits

Introduction to Real-Life Transformation

The journey to identify and change ghost habits can be deeply personal and transformative. While the concepts and strategies discussed in previous chapters provide the foundation for understanding and addressing these subconscious behaviors, real-life examples offer a powerful testament to the impact of such changes. In this chapter, we explore several case studies and personal stories of individuals who successfully identified their ghost habits and made lasting changes in their lives. These stories not only illustrate the challenges and triumphs of habit change but also provide inspiration and practical insights for anyone on a similar journey.

Case Study 1: Sarah's Journey to Mindful Eating

Background:

Sarah, a 32-year-old marketing professional, had struggled with her weight and relationship with food for most of her adult life. Despite numerous attempts to diet and exercise, she found herself consistently falling back into unhealthy eating patterns, particularly during stressful times. Sarah realized that her eating habits were often driven by emotions rather than hunger, but she felt powerless to change them.

Identifying the Ghost Habit:

Through journaling and reflection, Sarah discovered that her ghost habit was emotional eating, specifically when she felt stressed or overwhelmed. She noticed that she would often reach for comfort foods, such as chips and sweets, after a long day at work or when dealing with personal challenges. This habit had become so ingrained that she didn't even recognize it as a coping mechanism until she began paying closer attention to her behaviors.

The Process of Change:

Sarah decided to approach her ghost habit with mindfulness. She began practicing mindful eating, which involved paying close attention to her hunger cues, eating slowly, and savoring each bite. She also started keeping a food journal, where she recorded not just what she ate, but also how she felt before and after eating. This practice helped her identify the emotional triggers that led to her overeating.

To address these triggers, Sarah developed alternative coping mechanisms, such as taking a walk, practicing deep breathing exercises, or calling a friend when she felt stressed. She also began incorporating more nutritious foods into her diet and set small, achievable goals for herself, like preparing healthy meals at home and reducing her intake of processed snacks.

Outcome:

Over time, Sarah's relationship with food transformed. She no longer turned to food for comfort but instead found healthier ways to manage her emotions. As a result, she lost weight, felt more energetic, and experienced a significant improvement in her overall well-being. More importantly, she gained a sense of control over her eating habits, which had previously felt overwhelming and unmanageable.

Lessons Learned:

Sarah's story illustrates the power of mindfulness and self-awareness in breaking ghost habits. By identifying the emotional triggers behind her eating patterns and developing healthier coping mechanisms, she was able to make lasting changes in her life. Her journey underscores the significance of establishing achievable, incremental goals and recognizing each step forward as a meaningful accomplishment.

Case Study 2: James's Shift from Procrastination to Productivity

Background:

James, a 28-year-old software engineer, had always been a chronic procrastinator. Despite being highly capable and successful in his career, he struggled with completing tasks on time and often found himself working late into the night to meet deadlines. This habit not only affected his work-life balance but also caused significant stress and anxiety.

Identifying the Ghost Habit:

After recognizing the toll that procrastination was taking on his life, James decided to dig deeper into the root causes of his behavior. Through reflection and conversations with a mentor, he realized that his procrastination was driven by a fear of failure and perfectionism. He often delayed starting tasks because he was afraid he wouldn't be able to complete them perfectly, which led to a cycle of avoidance and last-minute panic.

The Process of Change:

James began addressing his ghost habit by breaking down his tasks into smaller, more manageable steps. Instead of focusing on completing an entire project, he set micro-goals for each day, such as writing a draft or outlining his ideas. This approach helped him overcome the initial hurdle of getting started and made the tasks feel less daunting.

He also implemented a technique called the "Pomodoro Technique," where he worked in short, focused intervals of 25 minutes, followed by a 5-minute break. This method allowed him to maintain his focus and build momentum without feeling overwhelmed by the size of the task.

To combat his perfectionism, James adopted a growth mindset, reminding himself that it was okay to make mistakes and that progress was more important than perfection. He also sought feedback from colleagues earlier in the process, which helped him refine his work gradually rather than striving for perfection from the start.

Outcome:

James's approach to work changed dramatically. By breaking tasks into smaller steps and using time management techniques, he was able to complete his work more efficiently and with less stress. His productivity increased, and he found that he had more free time to pursue hobbies and spend with loved ones. Most importantly, he no longer felt paralyzed by the fear of failure and was able to approach his work with greater confidence and a positive attitude.

Lessons Learned:

James's story demonstrates the effectiveness of breaking down tasks into smaller steps and using time management techniques to overcome procrastination. It also highlights the importance of challenging perfectionism and embracing a growth mindset. By addressing the underlying fears driving his procrastination, James was able to replace his ghost habit with more productive and positive behaviors.

Case Study 3: Emily's Transformation in Social Relationships

Background:

Emily, a 40-year-old teacher, had always struggled with social anxiety. She found it difficult to engage in conversations, often feeling self-conscious and afraid of being judged. As a result, she avoided social situations whenever possible and felt isolated from her peers. Her ghost habit of withdrawing from social interactions had become a significant barrier to building meaningful relationships.

Identifying the Ghost Habit:

Through therapy and self-reflection, Emily realized that her social anxiety was rooted in negative self-perceptions and a fear of rejection. Her ghost habit of avoiding social situations was a way to protect herself from potential embarrassment or failure. However, this habit only reinforced her feelings of isolation and prevented her from forming connections with others.

The Process of Change:

Emily decided to confront her social anxiety by gradually exposing herself to social situations in a controlled and supportive manner. She started by setting small, achievable goals, such as attending a social event for just 15 minutes or initiating a conversation with a colleague during lunch. Each time she successfully completed one of these goals, she celebrated the achievement and reflected on the positive outcomes.

To further support her progress, Emily practiced mindfulness techniques to manage her anxiety in the moment. She learned to recognize the physical sensations of anxiety, such as a racing heart or sweaty palms, and used deep breathing exercises to calm her nerves. She also worked on challenging her negative self-talk, replacing thoughts like "They won't like me" with more positive affirmations like "I have something valuable to contribute."

Emily also sought support from a close friend, who accompanied her to social events and provided encouragement. This support system helped her feel more comfortable and confident as she gradually expanded her social circle.

Outcome:

Over time, Emily's social anxiety diminished, and she became more comfortable in social settings. She formed new friendships, reconnected with old acquaintances, and even began hosting small gatherings at her home. Her newfound confidence in social situations spilled over into other areas of her life, enhancing her overall sense of well-being and happiness.

Lessons Learned:

Emily's journey illustrates how incremental exposure combined with mindfulness can be transformative in managing and ultimately overcoming social anxiety. By taking small, deliberate steps toward confronting her fears, and staying fully present in each moment, she was able to reduce her anxiety and build confidence in social settings over time. Her experience shows that with patience and self-awareness, it is possible to break free from the limitations of social anxiety.

By setting small, achievable goals and challenging her negative self-perceptions, she was able to break free from the ghost habit of avoidance and build meaningful relationships. Her experience also underscores the importance of seeking support from others and celebrating progress, no matter how small.

Case Study 4: David's Path to Financial Stability

Background:

David, a 45-year-old accountant, had always struggled with managing his finances. Although he had a steady income, he struggled to make ends meet, frequently relying on credit cards to manage unforeseen expenses between paychecks. His ghost habit of impulsive spending and avoiding budgeting had left him in a cycle of financial stress and uncertainty.

Identifying the Ghost Habit:

David recognized that his financial habits were driven by a lack of planning and emotional spending. He often made impulsive purchases to cope with stress or boredom, and he avoided creating a budget because it felt restrictive and overwhelming. This ghost habit had become a significant obstacle to achieving financial stability and long-term security.

The Process of Change:

David began by educating himself about personal finance and budgeting. He read books, attended workshops, and sought advice from a financial advisor. Armed with this knowledge, he set clear financial goals, such as paying off his credit card debt, building an emergency fund, and saving for retirement.

To address his impulsive spending, David implemented a 24-hour rule: before making any non-essential purchase, he would wait 24 hours to decide whether he truly needed or wanted the item. This pause helped him avoid impulsive buys and gave him time to reflect on his financial goals.

David also created a budget that aligned with his priorities and values. Instead of viewing the budget as restrictive, he saw it as a tool for achieving financial freedom. He tracked his expenses using a budgeting app, which helped him stay accountable and make informed decisions about his spending.

Outcome:

Over time, David gained control over his finances and began building a secure financial future. He paid off his credit card debt, established an emergency fund, and started contributing regularly to his retirement savings. The stress and anxiety that had once accompanied his financial situation were replaced with a sense of confidence and empowerment. David's new financial habits not only improved his financial health but also enhanced his overall quality of life.

Lessons Learned:

David's story illustrates the importance of financial education and intentional decision-making in overcoming ghost habits.

Lessons Learned: Applying Real-Life Insights to Your Journey

The stories of Sarah, James, Emily, and David illustrate the powerful impact that identifying and changing ghost habits can have on various aspects of life. From improving mental health and building stronger relationships to enhancing productivity and achieving financial stability, their experiences provide valuable insights that can be applied to your own journey of personal growth and transformation. This chapter distills key lessons from these case studies, offering practical guidance on how you can leverage these insights to overcome your own ghost habits and create lasting positive change.

1. The Power of Self-Awareness

Lesson: Identifying Triggers Is the First Step to Change

All of the individuals in the case studies began their journeys by becoming aware of their ghost habits. This self-awareness was crucial because it allowed them to recognize the triggers and underlying causes of their behaviors. Whether it was Sarah's realization that she was using food to cope with stress, or James's understanding that his procrastination was fueled by a fear of failure, identifying these triggers was the first step in breaking the cycle.

How to Apply This Lesson:

Practice Mindful Observation:

Pay close attention to your daily habits, particularly those that seem automatic or emotionally driven. Notice when you engage in these behaviors and what triggers them—whether it's a specific time of day, a particular emotion, or a certain environment.

Use Journaling as a Tool:

Keep a journal where you record your thoughts, feelings, and actions throughout the day. Look for patterns and recurring themes that might indicate the presence of ghost habits. Journaling can help you uncover triggers that you may not have been consciously aware of.

Reflect Regularly:

Set aside time each week to reflect on your habits and behaviors. Consider asking yourself reflective questions such as, "Are there any habits that I might be overlooking?" or "What specific triggers seem to prompt negative behaviors?" Regularly practicing introspection can significantly boost your self-awareness, helping you pinpoint specific areas in your life that require growth and attention. By consistently reflecting on your thoughts and behaviors, you can uncover patterns and take proactive steps toward self-improvement.

2. The Importance of Setting Small, Achievable Goals

Lesson: Breaking Down Big Goals into Smaller Steps Increases Success

One of the most consistent themes across the case studies is the effectiveness of setting small, manageable goals. Sarah, James,

Emily, and David all started with micro-goals that were easy to achieve and built momentum over time. This approach not only made their goals feel less overwhelming but also provided them with a series of small wins that reinforced their progress and motivated them to keep going.

How to Apply This Lesson:

Start with Micro-Goals:

Identify the larger habit or behavior you want to change and break it down into smaller, more achievable steps. For example, if your goal is to exercise regularly, start with a goal of just 10 minutes of physical activity each day. Once this becomes a habit, gradually increase the duration or intensity.

Celebrate Small Wins:

Each time you achieve a micro-goal, take a moment to celebrate your success. This could be as simple as acknowledging your progress with a positive affirmation or treating yourself to something enjoyable. Celebrating small wins helps to reinforce positive behavior and builds confidence in your ability to achieve larger goals.

Be Patient and Persistent:

Remember that lasting change takes time, and it's okay to progress slowly. Focus on consistency rather than speed, and be patient with yourself as you work toward your goals. Persistence is key to making small steps add up to significant, long-term change.

3. The Value of Mindfulness and Emotional Regulation

Lesson: Mindfulness Helps Manage Emotional Triggers and Builds Resilience

In the case studies, mindfulness played a critical role in helping individuals manage their emotional triggers and develop healthier coping mechanisms. For Sarah, mindfulness helped her recognize when she was eating out of stress rather than hunger. Emily used mindfulness techniques to manage her social anxiety and become more comfortable in social situations. By practicing mindfulness, they were able to respond to their emotions more thoughtfully and avoid falling back into negative habits.

How to Apply This Lesson:

Incorporate Mindfulness into Your Routine:

Set aside time each day for mindfulness practices, such as deep breathing, meditation, or mindful observation. These practices help you stay present and aware of your thoughts and emotions, making it easier to manage triggers as they arise.

Respond, Don't React:

When you notice an emotional trigger, pause and take a deep breath before responding. Take a moment to ask yourself, "What emotions am I experiencing right now?" and "How can I best respond to these feelings?" This brief pause can stop you from reacting on impulse and guide you toward making a more thoughtful and constructive choice.

Develop Healthy Coping Mechanisms: Identify healthier ways to cope with your emotions, such as exercise, creative activities, or talking to a trusted friend. These alternatives can help you manage stress, anxiety, or other emotions without resorting to negative habits.

4. The Role of Support Systems

Lesson: Accountability and Support from Others Enhance Success

Another key takeaway from the case studies is the importance of support systems in sustaining habit change. James benefited from the guidance of a mentor, Emily leaned on a close friend for encouragement, and David sought advice from a financial advisor. These support systems provided accountability, encouragement, and valuable insights that helped them stay on track and overcome obstacles.

How to Apply This Lesson:

Build a Support Network:

Surround yourself with people who are supportive of your goals and willing to hold you accountable. You can share your goals with those in your inner circle, such as close friends, family, coworkers, or even seek guidance from a professional like a coach or therapist. Explain your objectives clearly and discuss how they can assist you in staying motivated and on track.

Join a Community:

Explore the possibility of becoming part of a group or community where members share common objectives. Whether it's a fitness class, a support group, or an online forum, being part of a community provides a sense of belonging and mutual encouragement. You can share your experiences, learn from others, and stay motivated by seeing the progress of those around you.

Regular Check-Ins:

Set up consistent meetings with your accountability partner or support group to regularly track your progress and stay on course. These check-ins provide an opportunity to discuss your progress, celebrate successes, and address any challenges you're facing. Consistent communication helps keep you focused and committed to your goals.

5. *The Power of Positive Reinforcement*

Lesson: Positive Reinforcement Encourages Consistent Behavior Change

Positive reinforcement was a common strategy used by the individuals in the case studies to encourage consistent behavior change. David used the 24-hour rule to curb impulsive spending and rewarded himself with small treats when he stuck to his budget. Sarah celebrated her mindful eating practices with non-food rewards, and James recognized his productivity with short breaks and personal rewards.

How to Apply This Lesson:

Identify Meaningful Rewards:

Select rewards that genuinely resonate with you and inspire your motivation.. These rewards don't have to be extravagant; they could be simple pleasures like enjoying a favorite activity, taking a relaxing bath, or indulging in a small treat. The key is to choose something that you genuinely look forward to and that reinforces your positive behavior.

Use Immediate Rewards:

Provide yourself with immediate rewards after completing the desired behavior. For example, if you're trying to establish a habit of exercising, reward yourself with a relaxing activity right after your workout. Receiving immediate rewards reinforces the connection between your actions and their positive outcomes, increasing the likelihood that you'll engage in that behavior again.

Create a Reward System:

Consider setting up a reward system where you earn points or tokens for each successful behavior. You can redeem these points for more significant rewards after you've gathered a sufficient amount. A reward system adds an element of fun and motivation to the habit-change process, encouraging you to stay consistent.

6. *Embracing Setbacks as Learning Opportunities*

Lesson: Setbacks Are Part of the Process and Offer Valuable Lessons

Each of the individuals in the case studies experienced setbacks along their journey, but they didn't let these setbacks derail their progress. Instead, they viewed them as opportunities to learn and grow. James, for example, learned to adjust his approach when he encountered challenges with procrastination, and Emily used setbacks as opportunities to practice self-compassion and resilience.

How to Apply This Lesson:

Expect Setbacks:

Recognize that setbacks are a normal part of the habit-change process. Rather than viewing them as failures, see them as opportunities to learn more about yourself and your habits. Adopting this new perspective empowers you to maintain motivation and bounce back stronger when confronted with obstacles.

Analyze and Adjust:

When a setback occurs, take time to analyze what happened. What triggered the setback? How did you respond? What could you do differently next time? Use these insights to adjust your approach and strengthen your strategies for overcoming similar challenges in the future.

Practice Self-Compassion:

Be kind to yourself when setbacks occur. Avoid self-criticism and instead, focus on the progress you've made and the lessons you've learned. Remember that personal growth is a journey, and setbacks are simply part of that process.

7. Aligning Habits with Personal Values and Goals

Lesson: Habits Are More Sustainable When They Align with Your Core Values

A critical factor in the success of the individuals in the case studies was their ability to align their new habits with their personal values and long-term goals. David's commitment to financial stability was driven by his desire for security and peace of mind, while Sarah's shift to mindful eating was motivated by her value of self-care and well-being.

How to Apply This Lesson:

Clarify Your Values:

Take a moment to deeply consider your fundamental beliefs and the principles that guide your life. Reflect on what truly holds significance for you, shaping the person you want to be and the legacy you wish to leave behind. These values could include health, family, personal growth, financial security, or creativity. After recognizing your core values, let them serve as a compass for defining your goals and cultivating new habits.

Set Value-Driven Goals:

Ensure that your goals align with your values. When your goals are connected to what you truly care about, you're more likely to stay committed to them. For example, if health is a core value, setting a goal to exercise regularly or eat healthier will feel more meaningful and motivating.

Revisit Your Goals Regularly:

Regularly assess your goals to ensure they still align with your values and long-term objectives. As your life circumstances and priorities change, your goals and habits may need to be adjusted accordingly. Staying in tune with your values helps you maintain a sense of purpose and direction in your habit-change journey.

Conclusion

The stories of Sarah, James, Emily, and David offer valuable lessons that can be applied to your own journey of identifying and changing ghost habits. By cultivating self-awareness, setting small and achievable goals, practicing mindfulness, building a support system, using positive reinforcement, embracing setbacks as learning opportunities, and aligning your habits with your core values, you can create lasting positive change in your life. These lessons serve as a roadmap for overcoming the challenges of habit change and achieving the personal growth, fulfillment, and well-being that come from living a more intentional and purposeful life. As you embark on your own journey, remember that change is a process, and each step you take brings you closer to the life you envision.

Interactive Exercises: Applying Lessons from Real-Life Transformations

The stories of individuals who have successfully identified and changed their ghost habits provide powerful insights into the process of personal transformation. However, simply reading about these experiences is not enough. To truly benefit from these lessons, it's important to actively engage with the material and apply the concepts to your own life. This section includes a series of interactive exercises and reflective questions designed to help you do just that. These exercises will guide you in identifying your own ghost habits, setting meaningful goals, building support systems, and creating sustainable changes in your life.

Exercise 1: Identifying Your Ghost Habits
Objective:

To develop self-awareness by identifying the ghost habits that may be influencing your behavior.

Instructions:

Reflect on Your Daily Routine:

Take a moment to think about your daily routine, from the moment you wake up to the time you go to bed. Write down all the habits and behaviors that you engage in automatically, without much conscious thought.

Identify Emotional Triggers:

Consider the emotions you experience throughout the day. Are there specific situations that trigger certain behaviors? For example, do you find yourself snacking when you're stressed or checking your phone when you're bored? Write down any emotional triggers that seem to prompt automatic behaviors.

Look for Patterns:

Review your list of daily habits and emotional triggers. Are there any patterns or recurring themes? Do certain habits appear to be linked to specific emotions or situations? Highlight any habits that you suspect might be ghost habits—those that operate subconsciously and may not be serving your best interests.

Reflective Questions:

- Which of these habits do I feel in control of, and which seem to happen automatically?

- How do these habits make me feel afterward? Do they contribute positively or negatively to my well-being?

- What might be the underlying reasons for these habits? Are they rooted in past experiences, emotions, or environmental cues?

Commit to Change:

Choose one ghost habit that you would like to focus on changing. Write down why you want to change this habit and what benefits you hope to gain from doing so.

Exercise 2: Setting Small, Achievable Goals
Objective:

To break down larger goals into smaller, manageable steps that can be easily integrated into your daily life.

Instructions:

Identify a Long-Term Goal:

Think about a long-term goal related to the ghost habit you identified in the previous exercise. This goal should reflect the change you want to see in your behavior and lifestyle.

Break It Down:

Break your long-term goal into smaller, more manageable steps. Ensure that each step is clearly defined, quantifiable, and realistic. For example, if your goal is to improve your eating habits, your first small step might be to replace one unhealthy snack with a piece of fruit each day.

Set Micro-Goals:

To make consistent progress, break down your larger goals into smaller, manageable tasks that you can complete on a daily or weekly basis. These smaller objectives should be simple and achievable, allowing you to build confidence and maintain steady momentum toward your ultimate goal. For example, if your goal is to exercise more, your micro-goal might be to do five minutes of stretching every morning.

Create a Timeline:

Establish a timeline for achieving your small steps and micro-goals. Be realistic about how much time you need to make these changes and be sure to allow for flexibility in case of setbacks.

Reflective Questions:

- What are some simple actions I can take today that will bring me closer to achieving my long-term goal?

- How can I make these steps as specific and actionable as possible?

- What obstacles might I encounter, and how can I prepare for them?

Celebrate Your Progress:

As you achieve each micro-goal, take time to celebrate your progress. Write down how you will reward yourself for completing each step and how these rewards will motivate you to keep going.

Exercise 3: Practicing Mindfulness and Emotional Regulation

Objective:

To develop mindfulness practices that help you manage emotional triggers and respond to situations more thoughtfully.

Instructions:

Mindful Breathing Exercise:

Start with a simple mindful breathing exercise. Find a quiet place to sit comfortably. Close your eyes and bring your attention to your breathing. Take a deep breath in through your nose, allowing your lungs to fully expand. Hold the breath for a few moments, then gently release it through your mouth, feeling the tension leave your body as you exhale slowly. Repeat this process for five minutes, paying attention to the sensation of your breath and letting go of any distractions.

Mindful Observation:

Choose a daily activity, such as eating a meal, brushing your teeth, or taking a walk, and practice doing it mindfully. Focus fully on the experience, noticing the sights, sounds, smells, and sensations associated with the activity. If your mind starts to wander, gently bring your focus back to the present moment.

Identify Emotional Triggers:

Throughout the day, pay attention to your emotions and how they influence your behavior. When you notice an emotional trigger, pause and take a deep breath before responding. Take a moment to reflect on your emotions and their underlying causes, and think about how you can choose a response that supports your personal values and long-term objectives.

Reflective Questions:

- What emotions tend to trigger my ghost habits? How can I manage these emotions more effectively?

- How does practicing mindfulness affect my ability to stay present and make conscious choices?

- In what situations can I apply mindfulness to help break my ghost habits?

Develop a Mindfulness Routine:

Commit to practicing mindfulness daily, whether through meditation, mindful breathing, or mindful observation. Write down when and where you will practice, and consider setting reminders to help you stay consistent.

Exercise 4: Building a Support System
Objective:

To create a support system that provides accountability, encouragement, and guidance throughout your habit-change journey.

Instructions:

Identify Your Support Network:

Make a list of people who can support you in your habit-change journey. These could include friends, family members, colleagues, or professionals like a coach or therapist. Think about how each person can contribute to your success—whether by offering encouragement, holding you accountable, or providing expert advice.

Reach Out for Support:

Choose one or two people from your list and reach out to them. Communicate your aspirations and request their assistance in helping you achieve them. Be specific about what you need, whether it's regular check-ins, feedback, or simply someone to talk to when you face challenges.

Join a Community:

Seek out groups or communities that align with your goals and interests. These could include local organizations, online forums, or social media platforms where like-minded individuals gather. Engaging in these spaces can provide valuable support and insights for your journey. Joining a community provides a sense of belonging and collective motivation, making it easier to stay committed to your goals.

Establish Accountability Check-Ins:

Set up regular check-ins with your accountability partner or support group. These could be weekly phone calls, monthly meetings, or even daily text messages. Use these check-ins to discuss your progress, celebrate successes, and address any challenges you're facing.

Reflective Questions:

- Who in my life can provide the support and accountability I need to achieve my goals?

- How can I be proactive in seeking out support and building a strong network?

- What role can I play in supporting others who are on a similar journey?

Reciprocate Support:

Remember that support is a two-way street. Be there for others in your support network, offering encouragement, advice, and assistance when they need it. This mutual exchange strengthens relationships and reinforces your own commitment to change.

Exercise 5: Embracing Setbacks as Learning Opportunities
Objective:

To develop resilience by learning from setbacks and using them as opportunities for growth.

Instructions:

Reflect on Past Setbacks:

Think about a time when you experienced a setback in your habit-change journey. What happened? How did you respond? What valuable insights did you gain from this experience? Write down your reflections.

Analyze the Setback:

Consider what triggered the setback and how it affected your progress. Were there specific emotions, situations, or behaviors that contributed to it? What could you have done differently to prevent or mitigate the setback?

Develop a Recovery Plan:

Create a plan for how you will respond to future setbacks. This plan should include strategies for managing emotional triggers, adjusting your goals, and seeking support. Write down your recovery plan and keep it somewhere accessible as a reminder of your resilience.

Practice Self-Compassion:

When a setback occurs, practice self-compassion by treating yourself with kindness and understanding. Avoid self-criticism and instead, focus on what you can learn from the experience. Remind yourself that setbacks are a normal part of the journey and that each one offers an opportunity to grow stronger.

Reflective Questions:

- How have past setbacks contributed to my growth and development?

- What strategies can I use to recover from setbacks and stay on track with my goals?

- How can I practice self-compassion and maintain a positive mindset during challenging times?

Celebrate Your Resilience: Acknowledge your ability to overcome setbacks and continue moving forward. Celebrate your resilience by reflecting on how far you've come and the progress you've made, even in the face of challenges.

Conclusion

The exercises and reflective questions in this chapter are designed to help you apply the lessons from the case studies to your own life. By identifying your ghost habits, setting small and achievable goals, practicing mindfulness, building a support system, and embracing setbacks as learning opportunities, you can create lasting positive change. Remember that personal growth is a journey, and each step you take brings you closer to the life you envision. Use these exercises as a guide to deepen your self-awareness, strengthen your commitment, and empower yourself to overcome the challenges of habit change.

Conclusion

Ghost Habits: Breaking The Cycle of Self-Denial of Bad Habits has taken you on a journey through the hidden landscapes of your mind, exploring the subconscious patterns and routines that shape your daily life. These ghost habits, often operating beneath the surface of your awareness, can significantly impact your mental health, relationships, productivity, and overall well-being. But as you've discovered throughout this book, recognizing and understanding these habits is the first step toward meaningful change.

As we've explored together, ghost habits are more than just simple routines—they are deeply ingrained behaviors often rooted in past experiences, emotional triggers, and environmental cues. They can hold you back, keeping you stuck in cycles of self-denial, procrastination, emotional eating, or other behaviors that no longer serve you. However, by bringing these habits into the light of conscious awareness, you gain the power to break free from their grip.

The strategies outlined in this book are designed to guide you through the process of change in a way that is practical, manageable, and sustainable. By starting with small, actionable steps, you can create a ripple effect that leads to significant transformation over time. Whether it's setting micro-goals, practicing mindfulness, or building a strong support system, each step you take brings you closer to a life of greater intentionality and fulfillment.

As you reflect on the lessons learned from the real-life case studies presented in Chapter 6, you can see that lasting change is not only possible but also within your reach. The individuals who shared their stories with you faced many of the same challenges you might be experiencing now. Through perseverance, self-awareness, and the application of the techniques discussed in this book, they were able to overcome their ghost habits and create positive, lasting changes in their lives.

The journey doesn't end here. The tools and insights you've gained are just the beginning of your ongoing process of personal growth. As you continue to apply these strategies, you will likely encounter new challenges and setbacks. But remember, every setback is an opportunity for learning and growth. By embracing these challenges with a mindset of resilience and self-compassion, you can continue to evolve and refine your habits, making choices that align with your values and long-term goals.

Ultimately, the goal of this book is to empower you to live a more intentional life—one where your actions are guided by your conscious choices rather than by automatic, subconscious behaviors. By breaking the cycle of self-denial and addressing your ghost habits, you open the door to a life filled with greater purpose, joy, and fulfillment.

As you move forward, keep in mind the importance of consistency, patience, and self-compassion. Change is a process, not a destination, and each day offers a new opportunity to make progress, no matter how small. Acknowledge your achievements, grow from your challenges, and remain dedicated to the journey of personal growth and development.

Thank you for embarking on this journey with me. I hope the insights and strategies shared in this book will continue to serve you well as you work towards creating the life you truly desire. Remember, the power to change is within you—one small step at a time.

About the Author

Dr. Steve Miller is a renowned psychologist, author, and speaker, specializing in the study of human behavior, habit formation, and personal transformation. Dr. Miller, a seasoned psychologist with more than two decades of expertise, has committed his professional journey to guiding individuals in overcoming self-limiting habits and behaviors. His work focuses on empowering people to break these cycles and embrace a more purposeful and enriched life. Through his extensive experience, Dr. Miller has helped countless individuals make lasting positive changes, leading to personal growth and fulfillment.

Born and raised in Chicago, Illinois, Dr. Miller developed an early interest in understanding what drives human behavior. He pursued his passion by earning a Bachelor's degree in Psychology from the University of Chicago, followed by a Ph.D. in Clinical Psychology from Northwestern University. His academic research focused on the intricate mechanisms of habit formation and the impact of subconscious behaviors on mental health and well-being.

Throughout his career, Dr. Miller has worked with a diverse range of clients, from high-performing executives to individuals struggling with addiction. His groundbreaking approach combines traditional psychological theories with practical strategies for real-world application. Dr. Miller is particularly known for his ability to make complex psychological concepts accessible and actionable for a broad audience.

Dr. Miller's work has been featured in numerous publications, including Psychology Today and The Huffington Post, and he has been a guest on various television and radio programs, where he shares his insights on habit change, mindfulness, and personal growth. He is a sought-after speaker at conferences and workshops around the world, where he inspires audiences with his engaging and down-to-earth style.

In his latest book, Ghost Habits: Breaking The Cycle of Self-Denial of Bad Habits, Dr. Miller delves into the hidden routines that subconsciously control our lives. Drawing from years of research and clinical practice, he offers readers a clear roadmap for identifying and overcoming these "ghost habits." Through his compassionate guidance, Dr. Miller helps readers take small, manageable steps toward meaningful change, leading to improved mental health, stronger relationships, and greater personal fulfillment.

When he's not writing or speaking, Dr. Miller enjoys spending time with his family, hiking in the mountains, and practicing mindfulness meditation. He lives with his wife, Karen, and their two children in Boulder, Colorado, where he continues to explore new ways to help people unlock their full potential and lead happier, healthier lives.

Dr. Steve Miller's mission is simple: to empower individuals to take control of their lives by breaking free from the subconscious habits that hold them back, allowing them to live with greater intention, purpose, and joy.

Disclaimer

The information contained in Ghost Habits: Breaking The Cycle of Self-Denial of Bad Habits is intended for educational and informational purposes only. It is not intended as a substitute for professional advice, diagnosis, or treatment. Always seek the advice of your physician, psychologist, or other qualified health provider with any questions you may have regarding a medical condition, mental health issue, or other concerns.

The author, Dr. Steve Miller, and the publisher make no representations or warranties of any kind regarding the accuracy, applicability, or completeness of the contents of this book. The strategies, techniques, and suggestions presented in this book are intended to be used as tools for self-improvement and should be applied at the reader's discretion and risk. The author and publisher are not liable for any losses or damages resulting from the use of the information provided.

Individual results may vary, and the information provided in this book may not be suitable for everyone. Readers are encouraged to consult with a qualified professional before implementing any of the strategies discussed in this book, especially if they have underlying health conditions, mental health concerns, or other personal circumstances that may require specialized care.

The case studies and personal stories included in this book are either based on real-life experiences with details altered to protect the individuals' privacy or are entirely fictional. Any resemblance to actual persons, living or dead, or actual events is purely coincidental.

By reading this book, you acknowledge that you understand and accept this disclaimer.

Copyright

Ghost Habits: Breaking The Cycle of Self-Denial of Bad Habits

Copyright © 2024 by Dr. Steve Miller

All rights reserved.